LESLIE B. FLYNN

A native of Canada, Leslie B. Flynn received all of his higher education in the United States, after graduating from high school and business college in Hamilton, Ontario, Canada. He is a graduate of the Moody Bible Institute and Wheaton College (B.A.). From the Chicago area he moved to Pennsylvania where he received his B.D. degree at Eastern Baptist Theological Seminary in Philadelphia and his A.M. in Philosophy from the University of Pennsylvania.

He pastored the Bethlehem Baptist Church of St. Clair, Pennsylvania, from 1944 to 1949. In 1949 he assumed the pastorate of the Grace Conservative Baptist Church in Nanuet, New York, where he is still carrying on an effective ministry.

He has also been active in journalistic and educational circles, acting as regional editor of *Christian Life* Magazine since 1944, writing more than 200 articles for religious publications, and serving as an instructor in journalism in Nyack Missionary College since 1951. He is now Assistant Professor of Journalism in that school. He recently recorded an album for the Audio Bible of America, Williamsport, Pennsylvania.

Mr. Flynn is also the author of *Did I Say That?* published by Broadman Press in 1959 and now in its second printing. His wife, Bernice Carlson Flynn, is Family Editor of *Christian Life* Magazine.

Your God and Your Gold

CONTENTS

Your God
and Your Gold

by
LESLIE B. FLYNN

ZONDERVAN PUBLISHING HOUSE
GRAND RAPIDS, MICHIGAN

Printed in the United States of America

DEDICATED

To my seven daughters,

LINNEA; JANNA; MARILEE; ANNILEE;
DONNA; CAROL; *and* SUSAN

Who have taught me so many things

Money Talks — But What Does It Say?

1

Money Talks — But What Does It Say?

"The most sensitive nerve in the human body is the one that leads to the pocketbook," it has been said.

Two men out hunting deer were accidentally fired at by another marksman. One hunter was shot through the head. It didn't bother him a bit. He just plugged the hole up. But his pal dropped dead. Examination revealed that he wasn't hit in the body. He was only shot through the wallet.

Many people request ministers to preach on *Heaven,* or *Prayer,* or *How to Overcome Worry,* but rarely on *Money!* A minister visiting a reputedly ghost-ridden area in England was asked at breakfast if he had seen the family ghost the previous night. "Oh yes," replied the cleric, "he floated right up to the side of my bed. But he didn't stay long. He vanished the minute I mentioned I was going to take up an offering." Someone has suggested that "many men carry their wallet in their back hip pocket because their fondness for money is deep-seated."

The reason we are so touchy about money is that we are so closely identified with our dollars. Money represents us — our toil, our time, and our talent. Though it costs the government much less than a cent to print a one-dollar bill or a one *hundred* dollar bill, the real value of any currency lies in its symbolism. It stands for the brawn and brains of the man who earned it. Money is concentrated personality, or personality in coin. Someone has said, "Money is the tingling spinal column of man's life upon the earth." Another has put it, "Money is denatured manhood." Our picture may not be on any bill, but our person is certainly in it.

This symbol of self can be hoarded, selfishly spent, or sacrificially distributed. When a man gives it to any enterprise, he is giving part of himself.

Once there was a Christian,
He had a pious look.
His consecration was complete
Except his pocketbook.
He'd put a nickel on the plate
And then with might and main,
He'd sing: "When we asunder part
It gives me inward pain."
—*Religious Telescope*

Because to touch our money is to touch us, the Lord often spoke on this subject. Of the thirty-eight parables uttered by the Master, roughly one-third deal with possessions. One out of every six verses in Matthew, Mark, and Luke discusses the right use of material goods.

Money is a sensitive subject. Yes, money talks. A common jingle suggested how it speaks to many people.

If money talks
As some folks tell,
To most of us
It says, "Farewell."

But money speaks in *many* ways. To say money talks is an understatement. Money not only talks — it *screams*. But what does it say?

MONEY DISCLOSES INTERESTS

An angel in Milton's *Paradise Lost* could, by a touch of a certain spear, reveal the true character of a person, stripped of all veneer and pretense. The way we spend our money over and above necessities provides a good key to our real self. We may not give money away, but money will give us away.

A newspaper writer said, "If a man's after money, he's money-mad; if he keeps it, he's a capitalist; if he spends it, he's a playboy; if he doesn't get it, he's a ne'er-do-well; if he doesn't try to get it, he lacks ambition. If he gets it without working for it, he's a parasite; and if he accumulates it after a lifetime of hard work, people call him a fool who never got anything out of life." Though the above judgments show how easy it is to jump at false conclusions, the fact remains that a man's wallet is a very revealing aspect of his life.

The man who flips the newspaper first to the financial page to find out how US Steel and other companies are doing probably has money tied up in stock. If a lady's annual expenditures include large sums spent for clothes, it reveals a strong interest in personal appearance. A young lady who uses every spare dime to buy jazz records gives away her yen for fast music. Where our money goes shows where our concerns lie.

A traveler in a large city noticed in the hotel lobby a map of the city marked with all important places of interest. Theaters, night clubs, libraries, airport, railway and bus stations, department stores, and restaurants were all spotted, but no churches. If examination of a person's budget discloses sums of money allocated for food, insurance, clothes, car, home, laundry, books, entertainment, but nothing for the church, it points up a lack of interest in the things of God, even suggesting that such a person is a civilized heathen. When the collection plate was taken to Mr. Dives for a missionary offering, he shook his head and whispered, "I never give to missions." "Then take something out of the plate," the usher whispered. "The money is for the heathen."

> I am a fifty-cent piece.
> I scarcely am any use in a grocery store.
> I am too small to buy half a gallon of ice cream.
> I am not big enough to get into a football game.
> I am too small to purchase a box of chocolates.
> When my master and his wife go out to dinner, I'm not fit
>   for a tip, but —
> Believe me, when I attend church
> I am considered *Some Money!*

Those who invest little money in the Lord's work divulge little interest in the Lord's work. Those who contribute little to the bank of heaven but heap up treasures on earth unmask their affection for earthly wealth. This world has a greater pull than heaven. A rich man conducted his friend over his vast estate and through his lavish mansion, proudly pointing out his valuable works of art and widely accumulated treasures. He expected to hear his friend's congratulations but instead he heard the warning, "Ah, these are the things that make death terrible!"

On the other hand, the man or woman who generously gives to the Lord's work betrays a love for God and His will on earth. A man was haled before the Bureau of Internal Revenue to bring proof of his large donations to his church. Able to furnish canceled checks for the full amount declared as contributions on his income tax form, he heard the examining agent exclaim, "You certainly must be sold on your church!" Money discloses our interests.

Money talks. Yes, it screams. When clutched tightly or hoarded away, it says, "The man who holds me is a miser. His eyes keep looking for that which bears my image. My soft, metallic ring sounds louder to him than the cries of widows and orphans and the wail of perishing multitudes. I crowd out his sympathy for his fellow men and his love for God."

When spent foolishly on pleasure, money screams, "That youth that bartered me sells his soul for a mess of pottage. He wastes his substance in riotous living."

Or money may scream, "A man used me for a bribe. He wants power. He thinks me all-important. I will become his master."

How much better when money, given for the Lord's work, says, "That man is interested in the spiritual welfare of others. I will supply food for the hungry, clothes for the destitute, and medicine for the sick, but best of all,

I will send the Gospel of forgiveness through Christ to the lost at home and across the ocean."

What does your money say about you?

MONEY DIRECTS ATTITUDES

"I can't get interested in missions," remarked a young man. "No," his pastor replied, "you can hardly expect to. It's like getting interested in a bank; you have to put in a little something first and the more you put in — of time, money, or prayer — the more interest grows."

If a man buys stock in American Motors, it fixes his interest in that company. Where a man has money invested, his interest will follow. Or as Jesus put it, "Where your treasure is, there will your heart be also" (Matthew 6:21). That is why we should not lay up treasure on earth but invest in the bank of heaven. If our riches are earthly, our attitudes will be earthbound. If our wealth is stored in heaven, we shall be heavenly minded.

A Christian who says he can't drum up much interest in his Gospel-preaching church will help solve his problem by giving generously to his house of worship. Then his money will be in the church. Automatically he will be interested in the place in which he has invested. A lady who couldn't get excited about foreign missions was invited to share in the support of a missionary to Africa. Overnight she developed intense curiosity and concern about the missionary there — his health, his family, his difficulties, and his work. A well-to-do man never gave much thought to a Christian college nearby. When he was invited to serve on the board of trustees, he began to contribute generous sums to the college. Suddenly he became vitally involved in that school.

Money can ennoble or debase, elevate or lower, enrich or impoverish. Our thoughts tend to dwell on that which we prize highly. If we spend money for "meat which perisheth" and satisfieth not, our whole energies will be centered in the temporal and transitory. If we dispense our dollars for "that meat which endureth unto everlasting life," we will think about, speak about, read about, live for that which is eternal and permanent. Right use of money will help us set our "affection on things above, not on things on the earth" (Colossians 3:2).

God promised that when His people brought gifts to His house He would open the windows of heaven and pour out an overflowing blessing (Malachi 3:10). One of the blessings of assigning our money to the Lord's house is the resultant concentration on spiritual matters. Occupation and preoccupation with God's work, whether in the church and its local outreach or in the missionary cause abroad, will keep the spiritual level high and even foster revival.

A collection taken in the reign of Josiah, king of Judah, and used for repairs on the house of the Lord fixed interest in a spiritual direction. Out of this financial outlay came the rediscovery of the law of Moses in the house of the Lord, repentance by the people as they heard the law read, reformations by Josiah ridding the land of idolatry, and the keeping of the Passover in a manner unparalleled in many previous generations.

The California gold rush of 1848 turned on a "yellow" faucet which poured over four hundred million dollars into American trade in the next decade. Providentially, an interest in stewardship surged to the fore in many major denominations around this time which furnished an antidote to covetousness, sparked substantial increases in missionary giving, and issued in revival.

Realizing the pitiful inadequacy of puny collections, church leaders offered prizes for the best essays on money. Winning essays were widely published. Catching the vision, ministers preached much on the subject. In Northern Ireland, the "Ulster Prizes" listed by a group of evangelicals offered fifty pounds for the best statement in favor of proportionate giving.

The Presbyterians of Scotland were stirred to follow suit. The "Glasgow Prizes" carried a tidy honorarium of one hundred pounds for the winning essay. By winning second prize, an obscure young preacher by the name of

Joseph Parker was invited to the pastorate of the famous London City Temple. The American Tract Society announced a premium of $250 for the best treatise on systematic giving. Finding it impossible to select the best of 172 manuscripts submitted, The American Tract Society chose four essays, giving the authors a sum of $100 each and publishing their works to join the growing quota of literature on the theme of Christian stewardship throughout America and Great Britain.

Major mission boards reaped from the widespread emphasis on giving, many of them doubling their receipts in the period from 1850 to 1865. And because money helps direct our interests, it is not surprising that spiritual revival followed this stewardship resurgence. At the height of this "money" awakening, the revival of 1857-58 broke out. On September 23, 1857, a meeting for prayer was called in a church on Fulton Street in New York City. The place became too small for the crowds who came, despite the fact there was no preaching, only prayer. (Incidentally, this famed Fulton Street prayer meeting continued each week-day for over 100 years.) The flame spread to Boston, Philadelphia, Washington, Cincinnati, Chicago, and hundreds of towns across the land. Thousands gathered in daily prayer meetings. The Spirit of God fell in conviction on ungodly men who, confessing their sins, found joy in the Christian life. Likewise England, Scotland, and Northern Ireland experienced an unusual awakening, unequalled since the days of Wesley and Whitefield.

Money invested in spiritual projects provides an entrance into the more abundant life.

Money Demands Worship

"How much money do you want?" a millionaire was asked. He answered, "Just a little more."

Money charms. Enamored by his first thousand, a man heads for his second thousand. Should he reach one million, he will always want a second million. "He that loveth silver shall not be satisfied with silver" (Ecclesiastes 5:10). The word most frequently translated *covetousness* in the New Testament conveys "the wish to have more."

Another word translated *covetousness* (Hebrews 13:5) means "love of silver." The first command says that we are to love God with all our heart, soul, mind, and body. Too often God does not have first place in our affections. Since we are constituted so that we must always worship something, some object will always clamor for our devotion. One of the chief rivals for our allegiance is money. Among all the idols of history, Mammon is one of the most persistent and appealing. How often love of money displaces love of God. Perhaps the commonest form of idolatry is money-worship. Covetousness is clearly called idolatry by the inspired apostle Paul (Colossians 3:5). No wonder the Decalogue, which begins by commanding love to the Sovereign, ends with warning against love of silver — covetousness.

Some gods have many names. The god of money is no exception. It has been known by all the following terms, mostly slang: dough, jack, rhine, velvet, palm oil, shekels, simoleons, gingerbread, moss, chink, dibs, rocks, plunks, bucks, bones, wad, mazuma, kale, long green, dust, insect powder, brass, chips, clinkers, mopuses, off, ooftish, yellow boys. This devotion-demanding deity parades under many aliases. As early as 1890, scholars listed no less than 130 English slang expressions for money.

Because men worship money, they will do anything in its service. For thirty pieces of silver, betrayer Judas delivered Jesus to the rulers. Grafter Gehazi pursued the healed Naaman to ask a talent of silver. The prophet Micah warned that the prophets divined for money. Sorcerer Simon offered Peter money for the Holy Spirit. The Roman soldiers who were terror stricken by the earthquake that opened the tomb of the risen Christ were given "large money" to say that Christ did not rise from the dead but that His disciples came and stole Him away. Governor

Felix kept Paul imprisoned in the hope that money would be given him for Paul's release.

John Milton wrote,

> Mammon led them on,
> Mammon, the least erected spirit that fell
> From heaven.

We sometimes become like that which we worship. The glint of silver may be reflected in flush of a hoarder's check or in the steel of his eyes as he lusts after money.

Money which should really be a means to an end becomes for many an end in itself. Its fascinating power deceives people until it becomes their master. Other values in life are throttled under money's dictatorship. A seventy-year-old recluse who dropped dead in his tiny, two-room living quarters in eastern New York state left a fortune of $50,000 in savings banks, bonds, and uncashed pay checks. Another $1,350, mostly in $100 bills, was found tucked away behind a section of door trim. He had no relatives in America, no home, no car, and when he died, his legs and feet were encased in burlap bags tied with manila twine. A rope held his trousers up. His all-dominating money-god forbad him to give attention to even the minor comforts of life.

The power money has over people can keep them from heaven. Jesus plainly taught that a camel can more easily pass through the eye of a needle than a rich man through the gates of heaven. He also warned that "no man can serve two masters: for either he will hate the one, and love the other; or else he will hold to the one, and despise the other. Ye cannot serve God and mammon" (Matthew 6:24). Many years ago in China, fear gripped the population of a city, for their army had given way before an attacking war-lord whose soldiers would soon be looting the area. The people headed for a mission compound run by an English missionary. They were carrying their belongings, looking for safety under a foreign flag. Though every light in the city was out, the men, women and children could be heard fleeing the terror of the night. When they reached the compound, not an able-bodied man was permitted to enter, because that would be an invitation to invasion. Those who were allowed in were not permitted to bring a single possession more than they needed, not a ring or little jewel, no money, just the plainest clothing required by decency and no bedding beyond the barest need. The purpose was to exclude everything that would tempt a looter. The three missionaries on the compound wanted to be able to honestly say to the attackers (who, though gripped by greed, would accept a missionary's word) that the compound was a place of poverty. Thousands of fleeing people came to the mission that night seeking safety. But hundreds, learning that admittance demanded giving up their possessions, turned away. They were unwilling to part with their worldly possessions, rings, jewels, adornments, silks, silver, scarfs. So mastered by mammon were they that these things would have to be torn from their hands at bayonet point.

Money mastered the rich young ruler. When the Lord dealt a blow to his idolatry, he went away still clutching his idol. It was then Jesus said, "How hardly shall they that have riches enter into the kingdom of God!" (Mark 10:23).

Someone has said that a little boy playing in a sandpile on the beach can have more fun than a man with a million dollars. The small fellow with his imagination is master of the sandpile. But the man and his imagination are mastered by his money.

Coolidge said, "Prosperity is an instrument to be used, not a deity to be worshiped."

MONEY DENOTES VALUE

Someone asked, "What is money?" A little girl piped up, "Why, it's to buy things with!" She hit the nail on the head. Money is a medium of exchange. Money stands for value. Money represents purchasing power. Money is a means to acquisition. The rich man is called a man of means. He has "the wherewithal."

Before money was invented, many items served as a medium of exchange. In early American life, pelts of otters and beavers and other furs were used. Centuries back, the Romans had the custom of dividing property with their children when they came of age. Often houses and land were difficult to divide. Thus, settlement was often made in cattle. Hence, valuable property came to be called *pecunia,* from the Latin *pecus* (cattle). When coins became the medium of exchange, the word *pecunia* was attached to all forms of money. Some early coins were even stamped with an image of a cow and actually represented the literal value of an animal. Our flexible monetary systems today cannot escape being called *pecuniary.*

Money does not have intrinsic value, but representative value. The amount of silver, lead, or zinc may not equal the current value of that coin, but because it was minted by the government or because a paper bill bears a governmental promise to pay, that coin or bill represents a specified value. That is why crooks like to counterfeit money. Incidentally, on the outskirts of Leeds in northern England stands a big building more tightly guarded than any missile installations or atomic plants. It is the Thomas De La Rue & Co., printers of paper currency for 92 countries in the world. They are constantly engaged in a battle of wits against counterfeiters.

In a course on "Great Books," an English professor asked a pretty brunette coed which book she would choose if permitted only one. The girl quickly answered, "A checkbook." Because money is a measure of value, a medium of exchange, and a means of power, we say of it, "Money talks." And we add, "It screams." This also explains why there is a saying, "Every man has his price." Also, "Money isn't everything, but it's far ahead of whatever may happen to be in second place." And, "Money is relative — I wish it were my relative." On the other hand, when deflation punctures the value of things, people may react, "Money isn't everything. It isn't even what it used to be."

Money in itself is neither good nor bad. What is good or bad is how we spend it. Its real worth is determined by the person who puts it to some use. Money is not merely something that jingles in our pockets or crumples in our wallets. Because it is an extension of personality, all money is blood money. "Holiness unto the Lord" can be written on coins, or "Horror to the evil one." Money may be sacred or sordid. It is either a mercy or a madness.

Money becomes tarnished by the way we use it. The Latin word *lucrum* meant wages or profit or gain, a highly respectable term. But people did sometimes stoop to dirty or dishonest methods to gain *lucrum*. Such conduct Paul rebuked when in the vernacular of his day he spoke against religious leaders who taught for *filthy lucrum* (Titus 1:11). His remark was not directed against money itself but against wrong ways of acquiring money, thus tainting it. However, the term "filthy lucre" has come to designate money in general, whether gained honorably or dishonorably.

Much money is soiled by the way it is spent. It can be used to bribe, to seduce, to poison, to damn. But it need not be grimy. Wealth can be used to enforce the golden rule as well as the rule of gold. It can send needy children into a fresh air vacation in the summer, transport doctor's tools and medicines to disease-ridden areas, and dispatch missionaries to the corners of the earth. Money can teach converts, heal the sick, and win the lost at home or abroad. Money becomes as lovely as the grace of God when a worshiper expresses his gratitude to God for all His blessings.

Says the poet,

> Dug from the mountainside,
> Washed from the glen,
> Servant am I or the master of men;
> Steal me I curse you,
> Earn me I bless you;

Grasp me and hoard me,
A fiend shall possess you;
Live for me, die for me;
Covet me, take me;
Angel or Devil, I am what you make me.

Money is both material and spiritual. That is why
Paul could swing from the soul-exulting subject of the
Resurrection in I Corinthians 15 right into the topic of
money. The first four words after the inspiration of this
chapter are, "Now concerning the collection" (I Corinthians
16:1). Gold and the Gospel are closely related. Pentecost
influenced property. Though some in the Early Church
condemned wealth, more generally it was held that property
should be used to assist the needy, particularly those in
the household of faith.

The pursuit of money ought to be — and can be — a
spiritual calling. Many people are unwilling to dirty their
hands with the task of securing funds for God's work.
Not so with Jonathan Blanchard, first president of Wheaton
College, who used to make frequent trips specifically to
ask wealthy people to make gifts to his college. The handling of mundane money is beneath some people. Their
interest rests on more spiritual matters. The duty of some
men may well be to make much money and give large
sums to the Lord's work. To bury the money-making talent
would be wrong. Money-making is not a sordid business
unless made so by sordid man.

On the contrary, motivated by love for Christ and
with the prospect of laying up treasures in the bank of
heaven, a person can exchange the coin of earth into the
currency of heaven. In an obscure parable, our Lord advised, "Make to yourselves friends of the mammon of unrighteousness; that, when ye fail, they may receive you
into everlasting habitations" (Luke 16:9). The material
and temporal can become spiritual and eternal by proper
giving. A man with a thousand dollars spends it on pleasure
and has nothing to show for it. Another man with the
same amount buys a thousand copies of the Bible and dis-

tributes them. A harvest of souls believe on Christ through the written word. Out of the "unrighteous mammon" the giver has made immortal friends for heaven. His thousand dollars has been transmuted into eternal value.

Someone has said, "Christianity is a *personal* religion — *purse-and-all.*"

Money reveals where our interests lie; it can direct our attitudes; it ever exposes us to the danger of worshiping it; and it represents value. Yes, money not only talks; "it screams."

God Made the Decimal Point

2

God Made the Decimal Point

A wife asked her husband, "Can you give me a little money?"

"Yes," he said, "how little?"

Often people approach the matter of their contributions to the church with the silent question, "How little can I give?" They ponder within themselves, "What minimum amount is expected of me by other members, the finance committee, the pastor?" If they should ask in sincerity, "What is the least the Lord wants me to give?" the Bible has an answer. The Bible teaches that we should give at least a tithe, which means a tenth, or ten percent.

Some object to tithing because they claim it is legalistic, belongs to Judaism, and was therefore abrogated by the cross. Objectors fall into two categories with opposite motives, one set bad and the other good. Those with the wrong motive oppose tithing because they wish to escape the duty of giving as much as ten percent of their income. Free from the law of tithing, a person can give as little as he wishes. However, even if tithing were legalistic, should not Christians under grace far excel a bare tenth? Anyone who tries to evade his responsibility of giving ten percent on the grounds that such a practice belongs to the Old Testament does not understand his superior privileges under the New Testament which out of gratitude should make him willingly and cheerfully give above and beyond the legal ten percent. Legalism is often just a cover-up for covetousness.

Those who object to tithe-teaching from good motive fear that such legal instruction may fool people into smugly thinking that when they have given a tenth they have done all God requires in the area of financial stewardship. Some are concerned lest an emphasis on tithing lead people to selfishly regard the nine remaining tenths as their own, thus drying up the springs of generous giving and undercutting the glorious doctrine of stewardship. To allay such fears, it should be pointed out that the tithe is just a beginning point for giving.

At Wheaton College stands a dormitory known as Williston Hall. This building was named after a man who clerked in a drug store because poor eyesight prevented advanced schooling. Through hard work, Williston came to own the store. He promised God he would never give less than a tithe. He pledged $500 a year (a good amount 100 years ago) for ten years to Christian activities. Even though it meant the loss of simple comforts from time to time, he kept his word. Then he began an ink business. As he prospered, he donated to Christian activity, not a mere tenth, but all except a small portion of his income.

Certainly God wants us to give more than a tithe. But somewhere in His universe He must have given us an inkling of a minimum amount at which we begin. The Bible teaches that He has established the tithe not only as a starting point, but also as a stepping stone from which we advance.

How easy it is to figure out ten percent. Just write down the amount of income, then move the decimal point one space to the left, and you have the answer. No adding, no subtracting, no multiplying, and no dividing except by shifting the decimal point. It is so simple that even a child can do it Yes, God made the decimal point.

THE PRINCIPLE OF TITHING

1. Tithing in Ancient History

A Church of England scholar, Henry Lansdell, wrote a massive work, "The Sacred Tenth," in which he summarized research in archeology and history concerning giving in the ancient world. He concluded that most ancient pagan peoples practised tithing.

Babylonian clay tablets tell how the temple and priests were supported by the tithes of all classes of the population. One of the greatest buildings in Babylon was the storehouse for the tithes for heathen worship. In some cases, the Babylonians offered a sixth of their increase to their gods. The ancient Greeks held it a duty to offer a portion of their property to their gods, usually a tenth. One Greek tyrant, in writing Solon, told how everyone was paying a tithe of his goods for offerings and sacrifices to the deities. The legendary kings of Rome offered tenths of their spoils to their gods, as did merchants, farmers, and soldiers right up to the time of Christ. As far back as 1300 years before Christ, some of the earliest peoples in Europe gave tenths to their religious leaders.

The above is but a fraction of the material presented by Lansdell to show that tithing was practised in the ancient world.

2. Tithing in Genesis

If tithing were known by many widely separated ancient peoples, how did they learn of it? May it not be that God revealed to our first parents this principle, traces of which persisted through ancient history? Then tithing would take its place among other elements of creation ethics, such as marriage, the family, labor, Sabbath rest and worship. From the beginning God taught the necessity of giving a portion of increase back to Him as a token of Lordship and an act of worship.

Some early Christian fathers and councils opined that Cain's sin consisted in failing to offer a full tithe of his increase. The Septuagint, the Greek translation of the Hebrew Old Testament, accuses Cain of failing to "rightly divide" (Genesis 4:7), implying to some scholars that Cain failed to portion out the tithe. The New Testament commentary on this episode says that Abel offered a "more excellent sacrifice," which more literally would be translated "a more abundant sacrifice" (Hebrews 11:4).

Though the tenth is not clearly stated as such in the story of Cain and Abel, specific mention of the tithe is made twice in Genesis. After his successful battle against the kings who had captured his nephew Lot, Abraham gave tithes to God's priestly representative, Melchizedek (Genesis 14:17-20). This tithe offering showed not only Abraham's devotion to God but also his recognition of the tenth as an obligatory payment to God.

The fleeing Jacob, after his vision of a ladder reaching to heaven with angels ascending and descending, vowed that if God would be with him, he would surely give the tenth to the Lord (Genesis 28:22).

Those who contend that tithing is legalistic and Judaistic fail to take into account that long before the Israelites received the law at Sinai, God made known to men the definite percentage of income which men were to give to Him. Nothing in the Bible record suggests that this primal law was ever canceled.

3. Tithing in Israel

Examination of Moses' law indicates that the Israelites gave more than a tenth of their gain, perhaps up to as high as twenty-five percent.

The first tithe covered the produce of the field and the increase of the flock. If an offerer wished to retain the tenth of the fruit of the ground, he could do so by paying its value plus one-fifth. The extra fifth would cover any shrinkage of value through exchange so that the Lord would not get "the raw end of the deal." An offerer would determine God's share of his flocks by having the calves and the lambs pass by him. With rod in hand, he would touch every tenth one. He could in no way contrive to change their order so that a good animal would escape tenth place. If he tried to alter the order, both the real tenth and the attempted switch would be the Lord's (Leviticus 27:30-33).

This first tithe was called the Levitical tithe because it was to be paid to the Levites. Promoters of God's worship, they received no inheritance in the Promised Land but were to be supported by the tithes of the people. A few months ago a pastor answered a knock at his door one spring day to find a Jewish friend, who had shown recent interest in church attendance, standing with a small box of tomatoes in his hand. Said the Hebrew, "The law commands us to bring the first fruits of our fields to our priest." Incidentally, if twelve tribes brought a tenth each to the Levites, the latter fared rather well. In fact their income would have averaged twelve tenths, or 120 percent, in comparison with each of the other twelve tribes. In other words, the Old Testament clergy received twenty percent higher salary than the average person in their congregation, a situation just the reverse to today's ministers' wages.

In the second tithe, known as the festival tithe, a tenth of the remaining nine-tenths of the firstfruits of the land was used to prepare a sacrificial feast at the sanctuary. If the place of worship was far, then this second tithe could be sold and the proceeds carried to the temple where it would be used to buy food, drink, and ointment (Deuteronomy 14:22-29).

Every third year this second tithe, instead of being eaten at the sanctuary, was to be placed in a public storehouse in the home town as a charitable fund to help the orphans, widows, fatherless, and strangers (Deuteronomy 26:12-15).

Israel wasn't always faithful in giving the tithe. Sometimes she religiously gave the tenth when her heart was not behind the gift (Amos 4:4). In the last book of the Old Testament, Malachi three times accused the people of robbing God through failure to tithe (Malachi 3:8-10). The promise of the copious blessings on the giver shows the high degree of value God placed on the tithe.

4. *Tithing in the New Testament*

Raised in a pious home, the Lord Jesus Christ undeniably tithed. His enemies never charged him with failure to tithe. Though He condemned the Pharisees for neglecting the weightier matters of the law while meticulously paying the minutest tithe on the smallest plants of mint, anise, and cummin, the Lord Jesus nevertheless maintained that it was right for them to have paid the tithe. He said in effect, "Don't leave undone the careful payment of tithes" (Matthew 23:23). Though the Lord's teaching on giving went far beyond the tenth-stage to glad, abundant, overflowing generosity, He did put His approval on the minimal tithe.

That Jewish Christians paid tithes can be safely concluded from their zeal for the observance of the law (Acts 21:20). Peter, who was called to answer for the minor infraction of Pharisaical law of entering a Gentile house, would certainly have been rudely jolted to accountability had he been guilty of failure to tithe. Paul insisted that he taught nothing contrary to the law to his Jewish converts (Acts 21:21). Had Jewish converts failed to tithe, they would have suffered severe and prompt censure. Though many Jewish converts like Barnabas went far beyond the tithe, for they gave all they had, no consistent Jewish believer could go below the tithe.

If Jewish Christians showed as much, and even more, love for Christ than they had for the law, would not Gentile Christians be instructed in the matter of the tithe? When Paul wrote to the Corinthians that ministers had a right to be financially supported by the church just as old dispensation priests received their living from the people of Israel (I Corinthians 9:13, 14), he was referring to tithes on which presumably the Gentile Corinthian Christians must have had some instruction. Later in the same letter, Paul enjoins each Corinthian believer to give proportionately, "as God hath prospered him" (I Corinthians 16:2). With all the background of teaching they had, this proportion would be easily understood to be the minimal ten percent.

No testimony of a single bishop in the history of the Early Church ever condemned or opposed the doctrine of tithe giving, or ever hinted that less than a tenth was the proper proportion to be set aside for God's service.

The late Dr. Harry Ironside expressed it thus, "The least a consistent child of God in Old Testament times could give was a tenth. Certainly as a Christian living under grace I shall not do less than was required of a consistent Jew. The tenth, therefore, will be the minimum, and I will give more according as God prospers me."

The Purpose of Tithing

1. Money to carry on the Lord's work

A little barefoot boy was taunted by children in his block. "You are a Christian. Why doesn't God tell His friends to send you some shoes?"

The boy answered, "I think God does tell them but they don't listen."

God's work requires money. Missionaries need support, the poor ask help, churches require financial backing, Christian radio and TV programs consume dollars, Christian schools demand huge sums to operate, and multitudinous organizations doing a special work for Christ cry for money. To underwrite His work, God does not rain down showers of coins nor cover forest and meadow with the rich green of dollar bills. God depends on His children to supply the cash.

God has a system. Tithing (and tithing plus) is God's way of financing His interests. How much money would a public school system receive if it depended on the passing of a hat at a local PTA meeting to foot its bills? How would our Federal Government make out if it derived its income to carry on national activities by taking up a collection at Memorial or Independence Day parades? The school system levies taxes in systematic fashion. The government operates on astronomical figures received in systematic channels. Is God less systematic or business-like? God has a system. One-tenth of our income should go immediately to His work.

God does not act by impulse. As day follows night, and harvest the seed time, so God operates by law. Similarly God does not leave the support of His work on earth to hit-and-miss methods. Impulse giving may secure a large sum on one occasion, but that amount will be dwarfed by a regular, systematic giving of the tithe over any extended period of time. When Ben Franklin was taken to hear a sermon delivered by the orator-evangelist George Whitefield to raise money for a particular charity, he was so impressed he emptied his pockets into the offering plate. But that amount, generous as it may have been, would pale into insignificance in comparison to the total of consistent, ten percent contributions over a decade. Worship must be intelligent, not haphazard.

Jokes before the offering will not be required in churches where people give at least a tithe. Humor has its permissible place even at collection time, but should not provide the motive, spark, or foundation on which appeals are made. A famous lady evangelist reportedly asked everyone who would give a dollar in the offering to stand, then turned to the orchestra leader and asked him to play "The Star Spangled Banner." The story is told of a preacher who wired every seat in his church to a button on the pulpit. Sunday morning he asked all who would give a dollar to stand, then pushed the button that shot a dose of electricity into every seat. The next day the sexton found three Scotchmen electrocuted. No such dubious methods need be employed where systematic giving is practised.

Neither would the offering have to be taken up as it was one Sunday night in a mid-western church where nearly a thousand were in attendance. Two guest preachers were present, one a six-foot cowboy in wild-west regalia, the other a short, slightly built minister wearing glasses. At a given signal during the song service, after explanation, both preachers ran through the aisles begging for dollar bills, seeing which one could collect the more. The cowboy with his big boots ran to the back of the church to collect a bill from an outstretched hand, then spotting a choir member wanting to give him a bill, strode the full length of the aisle to retrieve the money. The little fellow hollered, "Don't forget me. Who's got a bill for me?" Bedlam reigned for five minutes as each ran through the aisles grabbing bills. When it was over, not much over a hundred dollars had been collected, which amount could have easily been exceeded by merely passing the plate in most churches with a couple dozen tithers present.

Neither is there need for fund-raising schemes in churches which tithe. Some churches get in the junk business through rummage sales; others land in the dry goods business by selling aprons; others enter the bakery business by selling cakes; and still others intrude into the restaurant business by selling meals. Horace Greeley once received a letter from a lady saying that her church was in distressing financial straits. The congregation had tried all sorts of devices — fairs, festivals, suppers, mock weddings, and socials. Would he suggest something new to keep the struggling church from disbanding? He wrote back, "Why not try religion?" Tithing would help take "the oyster stew out of the church and put the stew in stewardship." Churches which tithe have few financial worries.

Some folks who try to raise money for the church by various devices are trying to evade their responsibility to reach down in their own pockets and shell out ten percent of their income. Many ancient pagans would have been ashamed to bring to their gods the small portions which many modern people give to their church. Others, unaware of the teaching on the tithe, are conscientiously striving to aid their church. Only when stewardship teaching is allowed to lapse are schemes concocted for raising money. When people follow the Lord's method of tithing, church leaders and ladies' groups are freed from preoccupation with money-raising problems for more spiritual pursuits.

Failure to tithe causes God's work to fall into disrepair and disrepute. When Nehemiah heard that his people had neglected to restore the worship and service of the Lord, he made a visit to Jerusalem and rebuked the rulers, "Why is the house of God forsaken?" (Nehemiah 13:11). Because money had not been contributed, the Levites had left the temple service to work in their fields to support themselves, so that public worship fell by the way. Thus the revival under Nehemiah involved the bringing of the tithe by the people with the resultant cleansing and reopening of the temple.

Maintenance of God's work demands tithing by His people. If we want His program to prosper, the Christian must give. Since God has established the local church to spread His word, it seems logical that the first tithe should be deposited in the local church treasury from which it can be channeled out into worthy missionary objectives. Rather than individually diverting his tithe to private though worthy Christian enterprises outside the church budget, the Christian should join hands in the support of the local church budget. Then from his beyond and above offering (for no Christian should stop at the tithe) he can respond in some way to the constant financial appeals from dozens of reputable and effective Christian organizations. Giving the tithe to the local church gives stability to the church and extends its program on a sound basis. Tithing makes a man a partner with God.

2. Acknowledgment of God's ownership

Though the tithe will help support God's work on earth, God's purpose in instituting the tithe goes far deeper. It is intended as an acknowledgment on our part that God is owner of all we have plus everything else in the universe. To give the tithe without this recognition is to give without proper worship.

Man tempted to consider himself the owner of creation is rudely jolted to the truth of God's sovereignty by the law of the tithe. If man were to select the proportion

due God, it would signify man's authority over his possessions. But God's assignment of ten percent as the minimum
ratio due Him safeguards man from the presumptuous sin
of claiming as his own the values so graciously loaned him
by the owner God. Tithe giving is one evidence of capitu-
lation to God's mastery. Right giving is part of right living. The living is wrong when the giving is not right.

To make a good salary and then drop a quarter on the
collection plate once a week is sacrilegious mockery. To
make a good salary and place a dollar bill on the plate is
just a tip to God. Many people move the decimal point
one space too far — instead of giving one tenth, they give
one-tenth of a tenth. And anything less than ten percent
is robbing God.

You can determine the *quality* of your offering by
your spontaneity and devotion, but God has determined the
quantity. Only when you give over the tithe do you really
give. Little Nellie was given a brand new silver dollar.
She asked her father to change it into dimes. "Why?" he
asked.

"So I can get the Lord's part out of it, daddy."

When it was changed, she took one of the ten dimes
and said, "There! I will keep that till Sunday."

When Sunday came, she went to church and dropped
into the offering plate not one dime, but two dimes. "Why?"
asked her father as he heard the second one jingle. "I
thought you gave one-tenth to the Lord."

"No, daddy, I said one-tenth *belongs* to Him and I
can't give to the Lord what is already His, so if I give Him
anything, I must give Him some of what is mine."

Because of this principle — that a tithe belongs to God
as an acknowledgment of His ownership and we aren't
really giving until after we have given the tithe — many
churches list the offering in their Sunday morning order
of service as "Tithes and Offerings." One pastor used to
call the ushers forward with this remark, "We will now
receive His tithes and our offerings."

Some excuse themselves from tithing because they say

they can't keep track of their income. But we keep a record of our income and submit it in writing to the Bureau of Internal Revenue annually. If we do it for the government we can do it for God. Were our government to enact a law that a citizen who would send to the capital at the end of the year a statement of his yearly income so that the state treasurer could send him by return mail a cash bonus equaling one-tenth of the amount of his reported income, most people would take pains to keep records so as to qualify for the bonus.

Another excuse offered by non-tithers is, "I can't afford to tithe. If I made more money, I could tithe." Such reasoning is self-deceptive. When our income is low, we feel we can't spare the tithe. But when our income is larger, we feel that a tithe is too much to give away. He who is not liberal with what he has fools himself when he thinks he would be liberal if he had more. What we would do with a lot is exactly what we do now with a little.

A little boy walking home from church with his mother declared, "When I get to be a man and have lots of money, I'm going to build a church in our country and a mission hospital on the foreign field."

"Are you sure you'll still feel that way when you get the money?" queried his mother.

"Oh, I know I will!" answered the boy confidently. "If I had any money now I'd give it, but I haven't any."

Just then he spotted a shiny round dime on the sidewalk. Before his mother had a chance to say "church" or "mission hospital," he shot into a nearby store where the dime was hurried across the counter to buy his favorite candy. Though willing to give mythical dollars that he was going to have some day, he was unwilling to give a part of the dime he had now.

When someone suggested taking up a missionary offering at a summer youth conference, another commented, "It's a shame to ask these young people to make gifts. They have no money." Yet in the nearby refreshment stand during the conference days, more than $1,000 was passed over the counter by those same poor young people to buy soft drinks, candy, and ice cream.

We can't afford to tithe? The real truth is — we can't afford not to tithe! Nine-tenths with God go farther than ten-tenths without Him!

If we are delinquent in making an offering to God, perhaps God will take up an offering from our pocketbooks. He may collect His due in the form of depression or war. Some slogans during World War II were thought-provoking. "Ten percent is the rent everyone must pay to keep the Axis off the land" was the pitch to get people to buy bonds. A popular song went, "I'm saving a dime out of every dollar and helping to save the U.S.A." One radio station used to have its announcers give time like this, "It's 6:45 a.m. Central War Time and war time means ten percent plus." Is there any significance in the ten percent figure? Could it be that because we did not give God the tithe, He took up a collection in His own way? Augustine once blamed the excessive taxation and the invasion of the heathen hordes into the Roman Empire on the people's neglect of tithing. He said, "Our forefathers abounded in plenty because they gave to God tithes. But now because our devotion toward God has receded, the imposition of taxes has advanced. We were unwilling to share with God, giving Him the tenth, and now the whole is taken from us. The taxgatherer takes from us that which Christ receives not."

How important to "Honor the Lord with thy substance, and with the fruit of thine increase" (Proverbs 3:9).

3. Effect on the giver

The main purpose of tithing is not to secure the tithe but to secure the tither. Someone has said, "Giving is not just a way of raising money. It is God's way of raising men."

Tithing cuts right through the core of covetousness. For a person to regularly and systematically and cheerfully set aside one dollar in every ten he earns and give it away to the Lord's work without inward struggle strikes blow after blow at the root enemy of man's soul, love of money, selfishness, and covetousness which is idolatry. The birth of charity speeds the death of covetousness.

One evening a denominational leader held a scheduled meeting in a village church to present Biblical giving and intelligent business methods in the church. Most of the men present earned a comfortable living. The speaker spoke of tithing, presented charts and diagrams, the weekly offering, and the duplex envelope system. But the men did not respond with any enthusiasm. The speaker went over the same ground, telling how successful the plan had proven in other village churches and showing how if adopted it would double the financial income of their church. Again the response was unenthusiastic. A shrewd looking farmer near the front leaned forward, pointed a long index finger at the charts, then drawled, "They's a ketch in it."

"I thought I made it plain," said the speaker.

"Oh, it's plain enough," said the farmer, whose shrewd eyes half closed as he continued, "but they's a ketch in it all the same. They's deceit in it; for I can see, if we adopt that plan, we'll be payin' out more money than we intend to give."

Because tithing makes a man give more than he wants to by nature, it is a good antidote to covetousness.

Tithing helps teach that it is more blessed to give than to receive. Not an emotional matter, but a habitual thing, tithing develops "giving habit tracks" just as the repetition of other acts creates habit tracks, making it easier to do those things again. Tithing makes it easier to give next time, and to give additional sums. Incidentally, to put one's tithe on the plate, a person will usually have to go to church, thus helping create the practice of regular church attendance.

Tithing demands that the giver give now while he is alive, not waiting to leave large proceeds in his will to churches and missionary societies. Bequests to Christian groups are excellent but are not substitutes for regular tithing during life. One rich man complained to his pastor,

"Why is it that everybody criticizes me for being miserly when they know that I have made plans to leave everything I own to charity when I die?"

The pastor told the miser a story about a pig who lamented his lack of popularity. Said the pig, "Everybody speaks kindly about the cow, its gentleness and kind eyes. Oh, I admit the cow gives milk and cream, but pigs give more. Why, we pigs give bacon, ham, bristles, and people even pickle our feet. Tell me why people don't appreciate the pig." A cow standing nearby replied, "Maybe it's because we cows give while we're still living."

Someone has summed up the spiritual values of tithing in the language of photography, "It focuses your heart on God, enlarges your concern for others, sharpens your thinking about spiritual matters, develops your interest in missions, puts into lovely frame your attitude toward money and reflects the Spirit of Christ, a self-sacrificing desire that seeks to give rather than receive."

Someone else has listed the things that most tithers will be surprised at:

1. The amount of money he has for the Lord's work.
2. The deepening of his spiritual life through paying the tithe.
3. The ease in meeting his obligations with the nine-tenths he has left.
4. The ease in going from one-tenth to larger giving.
5. The preparation this gives to wise and faithful stewardship over the nine-tenths that remain.
6. Himself for not adopting the plan sooner.
7. The peculiar joy that comes in counting the tithe sacred unto the Lord.

Though the Bible does not promise material prosperity to the tither, but rather spiritual blessing, the Lord always takes care of those who tithe. Dr. Russell Conwell, founder of Temple University and the Baptist Temple in Philadelphia, once asked for testimonies in prayer meeting of those who had tithed for several years. Six gave glowing witness to blessings received. The seventh to speak, a frail woman of seventy, reluctantly said, "I wish I could bear such testimony but I cannot. I have skimped and saved and denied myself through the years to keep a vow made many years ago that I would tithe my income. But now I am old, am losing my position and have no means of support. I don't know what I shall do." When she sat down, the meeting was closed in a depressing chill. The next day Dr. Conwell was lunching with John Wanamaker, founder of the Wanamaker department store. The latter said, "Dr. Conwell, I think you will be interested to know that our store is about to inaugurate a pension system for our employees. We have thought about it for years. Finally the plan has been worked out. We are about to issue our first life pension today to a woman who has served our firm for 25 years." Then he mentioned the name of the woman. It was she who had given the pessimistic testimony in prayer meeting the night before.

For over five years $100 has been on deposit in a bank in California which anyone could claim who tried tithing for one year and found that God didn't keep His promise to take adequate care of the giver. No one has claimed the money. The pastor of the church who made the deposit has renewed the offer with the promise to include the interest as well. One-third of his membership of nearly 500 tithes. None has shown any inclination to collect the $100.

A tithing pledge which has been signed by thousands of people reads, "God's Tithing Covenant I hereby accept, and I promise to faithfully set aside, systematically and regularly, one-tenth of my income, wages, increase or profit, to the Lord God, and will use my best conscientious judgment in disbursing it for the upbuilding of God's kingdom, and trust God to bless me as He has promised."

Can You Justify Your Expense Account?

3

Can You Justify Your Expense Account?

A character in the Li'l Abner comic strip once suggested that the government raise extra revenue by renting advertising space on its coins. The scheme never passed the suggestion stage. However, a real-life Indianapolis meat packer who didn't read Li'l Abner landed onto the same idea and into a lot of trouble. To announce the 17th anniversary of his company, meat packer George Stark ordered 80,000 silver dollars from Chicago on which he paid $240 freight charges. Then he hired fifteen girls to glue on printed stickers. On two consecutive paydays, his eight hundred employees took home their wages in anniversary-advertising dollars which they spread through Indianapolis stores, movies, restaurants, bars, and a few churches. Then the Secret Service stepped in to inform Stark of a law which imposes a fine for defacing U.S. coins with advertising — up to $500 for each coin. With a possible forty million dollar fine hanging over his head, Stark promptly apologized and offered to buy back his illegal coins. Feeling he had no criminal intent, the government agreed. Stark assigned eight office workers the difficult task of de-decorating the dollars whose soak-resistant stickers had to be pared off with a knife. When the story was reported in the papers, the meat packer had another $73,000 yet to find.

Though most people would not be guilty of doctoring up dollars in such a way, many Christians take God's money and mark it up for personal advantage. A stabbingly true-to-life cartoon appearing in a religious publication shows this caption at the top of the grave of Jim Elliot, one of the missionaries martyred by the Auca Indians, "He is no fool who gives what he cannot keep to gain what he cannot lose." Underneath is the drawing of a fancy, modern home with swimming pool, two late-model cars, a large yard with outdoor equipment, two TV sets, modern furniture, and on the patio sitting in a lounging chair a young husband who has just finished reading a letter handed him by his wife who stands by his side. They exclaim, "Another missionary appeal! We gave our tithe. Surely no one expects us to give more!"

To think that payment of our tithe discharges our financial obligation to God is a gross deception. Man's responsibility with respect to his money involves far more than ten percent. It encompasses the entire one hundred percent of his money. Not just one tenth belongs to God. Ten tenths are His!

God wants us to tithe. This acknowledges our recognition of His ownership of all our money. Because He owns the remaining nine-tenths, He wants us to administer this balance carefully. We shall be accountable some day for the way we spend the other ninety percent.

It is as though we have been given an expense account by the Lord. We must be able to justify the items we charge against it. Just as a traveling salesman would find it impossible to justify the purchase from his expense account of a fur coat for his wife and a bicycle for his boy, so many Christians should find it difficult to spend money with a clear conscience for extravagant and unnecessary luxuries. And just as a salesman would find himself in trouble for such practices, so many Christians will suffer shock, embarrassment and utter remorse in the day of reckoning when the Bookkeeper of the universe makes His final audit. The doctrine of stewardship involves far more than a tithe. It covers all our money.

GOD IS OWNER OF ALL OUR MONEY

In an ancient treatise on *Things* the writer says, "Precious stones, gems, and other things, found upon the seashore, become immediately, by the law of nature, the property of the finder." Though this pagan concept holds that man owns things, Biblical truth asserts the absolute ownership of Jehovah God who claims, "The silver is mine, the gold is mine, also the cattle on a thousand hills." Says the psalmist, "The earth is the Lord's and the fulness thereof."

In reality, man owns nothing. God is owner. Man may possess, but God is ultimate owner. Man may have title to possession of property which can soon pass into possession of another, all the time remaining in the ownership of God. A girl relates, "One day after my grandmother's death, mother brought home a pair of brass candlesticks. Sister Joan and I recognized them as the ones that had always sat on grandmother's mantel. We asked mother if she owned them now that grandmother was gone.

"Mother replied, 'Nearly a hundred years ago great-grandfather bought them. He thought they were his because he paid for them. But after a while he died and they came to grandfather. He thought they were his because his father left them to him. But after a while he died and Aunt Sue kept them for many years. But she passed away and they came to your grandmother. Now grandma is dead, the house is to be sold, and the candlesticks have come to me. Who really owns them?' "

The answer is obvious if we follow Biblical thinking. Different individuals possessed them, each for a few years at most. But even though possession changed from relative to relative, God was always the real owner. The Lord says, "The earth is mine; unto you it is given for a possession."

A New York law firm, engaged to clear the title to some property in New Orleans, hired a New Orleans lawyer to get the facts from the record. The southern lawyer wrote that the property could be traced back to 1803 when the United States had purchased the territory of Louisiana from France. The New York firm replied that he would have to go back farther. Later this letter came from the New Orleans attorney: "Please be advised that France acquired title from Spain by conquest. The Spanish crown obtained it through the discovery of Christopher Columbus, a sailor who had been authorized to sail by Isabella, Queen of Spain, who obtained sanction from the Pope, the Vicar of Christ, who is the Heir of Almighty God, who made Louisiana." Though the Pope's position in this chain may be questioned, the rightful ownership of Almighty God cannot be denied.

Debate recurs on the question, "Who owns the tidelands?" It may pose a problem as to whether state or federal government has the right to possess them, but it is God who owns them. The coal, timber, soil, minerals, and grain belong to God. Says the poet,

> Back of the loaf is the snowy flour
> And back of the flour the mill,
> And back of the mill are the wheat and the shower
> And the sun and the Father's will.
> — *Maltbie D. Babcock*

That we merely possess, not own, property is evident in the many ways we subordinate ourselves to higher authority. We have to pay taxes. In time of war, the government may seize our supplies and make payment in any amount it chooses. If fire threatens a city, the fire department may pour water on a man's house to protect adjacent buildings. If a man builds a new house, he must choose a site in keeping with the zoning ordinance, submit plans for approval to some board, and have the completed building inspected for approval before occupancy. When the government wishes to build a new highway or reservoir that will take some of a man's property, it has paramount right to buy it without the possessor's consent and at virtually whatever value the government chooses. Some people have exclaimed, "So burdensome are restrictions and taxes that I just couldn't afford to own property!"

WE ARE STEWARDS OF GOD'S MONEY

Someone has said, "Property is not an earthly treasure but a heavenly trust." God, the Owner, has entrusted His possessions to us, who thereby become His stewards. We must give an account of that which He puts under our care. We owe — not own!

The word *steward* conjures up in many minds the thought of a man who serves food on a train or ship. Its feminine counterpart, *stewardess*, makes us think of a trim, neatly attired, sweet dispositioned young lady who helps us on our plane trips. But its primary meaning is an officer or employee in a large family or on a large estate who manages domestic concerns, supervises servants, collects rents or income and keeps accounts. He is basically an administrator, supervisor, or manager.

In Bible times his status was that of a friend, a servant in a high and confidential capacity. Eleazar, Abraham's steward, ran Abraham's house and money, even taking his master's jewels on a trip to find a bride for Abraham's son. But steward Eleazar didn't own Abraham's house, money, and jewels. He only managed these things for Abraham. Joseph was made overseer over Potiphar's house, and all that Potiphar had he put into Joseph's hand. But Joseph didn't own his master's money; he just ran it for him and was accountable for the way he managed it. The Lord told the parable of a steward about to be fired who used his master's possessions to win friends who would therefore help him when out of a job. Though our Lord commended his zeal, but not his wrong, the point is that as a steward he was entrusted with his master's goods. The parables involving talents, pounds, and vineyards teach that God makes us stewards of pounds, talents, and vineyards, not as our own but on loan to us and for which we shall be responsible some day.

Jesus never taught that money was evil. God doesn't say, "Hands off the earth," but "Have dominion over the earth. Subdue it for My glory. Possess it for Me!" The Lord says to His stewards, "Trade herewith. Put these talents to good use. Increase My wealth." One parabolic steward was rebuked for hiding his talent instead of increasing it.

Money itself is not evil, but *love* of money is. Jesus never condemned the rich for having riches but for acting as if the riches were theirs. It is not wrong to want to earn money, if we realize the money is not really ours but His. It is not wrong to be rich, but to be a rich fool. A fool, whether rich or poor, is one who considers his possessions his own, inwardly saying, "*My* barns, *my* fruits, *my* goods."

Not ownership, but stewardship, the Christian faith teaches. Apart from the Bible, man is likely to think he is the owner of his money. Stewardship is not a natural human concept, and it won't be discovered by man's un-aided reason. When a rousing speech elicits a good offering, that isn't stewardship. Rather, according to the Scriptures, stewardship is the attitude of a Christian toward his pos-sessions. Stewardship is the recognition that God is owner of all economic value and, therefore, that private property must be administered as a sacred trust. Again, to have is to owe, not own! Stewardship pushes gold from the cen-ter of our life and puts God there.

When we give any money to the Lord, we only give what is really His. A little girl told her teacher that she was going to give her father a pair of bedroom slippers for his birthday. "Where will you get the money?" the teacher asked. The little girl opened her eyes like saucers, "Why, Father will give it to me!" The teacher thought to herself, "The father will pay for his own birthday gift." But father loved his little girl for her gift even though he paid for it. She hadn't anything in her possession that her daddy hadn't given her. We can't give to God anything but what be-longs to Him. "All things come of thee, and of thine own have we given thee" (I Chronicles 29:14).

One pastor used to pray before the offering, "We are owners of nothing, stewards of all." One church used to sing before the offering,

> We give Thee but Thine own
> Whate'er the gift may be;
> All that we have is Thine alone,
> A trust, O Lord, from Thee.   —*William W. How*

A little girl used to mark words she didn't know when reading. One day her mother noticed she passed the long word *stewardship* without marking it. "Do you know what it means?" her mother asked. "Oh, yes," the little girl replied. "It means that I've got it but that I must use it for someone else."

Unenlightened human nature, plus the Christian's carnal nature, say, "I've got it and I'm going to use it for myself." Failure to recognize God's ownership is to be guilty of embezzling trust funds.

THE TITHE IS ACKNOWLEDGMENT OF GOD'S OWNERSHIP

Mr. Tenant is a farmer who does not own his land, but rents from Mr. Master who lives in the city. By agreement, Mr. Master pays all the taxes and insurance on the farm buidings. Mr. Tenant has possession for an indefinite term of years, has full charge of the farm, raises the crops he likes best, markets them at his price, has full use of pastures, springs, and trees from which he may cut fuel for his own use and timber for repair on buildings, and occupies all buildings on the land. On proper notice, he is to turn over possession to the rightful owner.

As consideration for all these privileges, what does Mr. Tenant do? Does he merely show politeness to Mr. Master and his family when they visit the farm? Is he to leave a basket of strawberries or sweet peas on Mr. Master's porch when he drives by his house? Is he to wave a friendly hello when he sees Mr. Master in church? Is he to put in a good word for Mr. Master when his name is mentioned in the corner grocery store? Kind as these things are, they do not constitute the consideration necessary.

Mr. Tenant knows he does not own the farm. It has been in the Master family for several generations. He also knows that the one acknowledgment of ownership both equitable and legal is the payment of the kind of consideration named in the lease — rent. If he pays rent, all other acts of courtesy strengthen their good relationship. If he fails to pay, his pretensions of kindness have no meaning whatsoever. In addition, he will be forced off the farm.

Without discussing the economic angle of rent, the legal aspect involves the *acknowledgment of another's ownership.* Rent may be paid in money, produce, or service, but whichever the type, the meaning in the legal sense is acknowledgment that the land belongs to another. Payment of rent means the owner's title cannot be clouded by physical possession by the tenant. Rent safeguards the owner's property against the truth expressed in the saying, "Possession is nine points of the law."

The English word "rent" derives from the Latin *reddita,* from *re* and *dare,* literally, "to give again" or "to give back." The verb *render* has the same derivation and meaning. *Rent* is that rendered or given back.

Payment of the tithe is our acknowledgment that God is owner of all our material things. Singing hymns of adoration to God, saying nice things about God, going to His house once a week and dropping a dollar on the plate are fine gestures, but they do not fulfill our responsibility to God. Not till we have *rendered* ten percent of our income to God have we "paid the rent." All other acts of worship but evade our duty. Our Great Owner still says, "Why call ye me Lord and do not the things I say?" *Pray* and *pay* go together.

American Christians are not paying the rent they owe God. A glance at figures released by major denominations in the U.S.A. reveals that the average church member gives from 75¢ to $1.50 per week to the Lord's work, including both local church and foreign missions. A few smaller denominations have a per capita average of around $2 per week. One of the most serious blights on our country is our gross materialism. Vast sums are spent on unimportant items while God's interests are bypassed. We spend more on gum than on God.

To figure out the amount of the rent due God is so easy. (See the chapter, *God Made the Decimal Point*). Neglect of the tithe-rent is failure to acknowledge God's ownership.

THE REMAINING NINE TENTHS MUST BE SPENT WISELY

We must advance beyond the tithe. Some who give the tenth hold the mistaken philosophy that to honor God and pay the tithe is the whole financial duty of man. This impoverished view needs correction. Stewardship demands a careful administration of the other nine tenths as well. Though not necessary to give all, it is essential to consider all as God's and to administer all as His. Our title to some economic value is not as important as our attitude toward it. A man may respond willingly and generously now and again to worthy causes, but if he doesn't consider all his money as a trust from God, he may be a good fellow but he is not a good steward. The real test of a man's stewardship is not his sporadic giving or even tithe giving, but the use of the principal nine tenths. Someone has written,

> Nine dollars for me and one for the Lord;
> Somehow that seems very small
> When I think how He counted not the cost
> But freely poured out His all.
> Shall I stop giving a tenth, when He
> Has given Himself — priceless gift — for me?

1. We are on an expense account

A salesman starts a two-week trip on the road for his company. Along with credit cards, he is given $300 in traveler's checks for expenses. Along the way he uses his cards and checks to pay for hotel, food, gas, and necessary bills. Should he use company money to buy personal items, he would find himself in a predicament.

We are on an expense account from God. He has entrusted us with money for certain necessary and legitimate expenses. We shall be accountable for any wasteful expenditures.

The head of a family cannot say, "Shall I, or shall I not, support my family?" It isn't the father's money to do as he pleases. Top priority on the expense account is care for wife, children, and close, dependent relatives. "The children ought not to lay up for the parents, but the parents

for the children" (II Corinthians 12:14). Speaking specifically of widows but indirectly of other dependents,
Paul warns, "If any provide not for his own, and specially
for those of his own house, he hath denied the faith, and is
worse than an infidel" (I Timothy 5:8).

Family support includes food, clothing, housing, medical and dental care, insurance, educational saving, recrea-
tion, cultural pursuits like concerts or music lessons, car,
and prudent foresight for a rainy day. John Wesley, with
his strict views on money, nevertheless permitted reason-
able provision for one's dependents. Why would it not
also be permissible to invest modestly in the stock of company enterprises, without which our great American economy and high standard of living would never have been
possible?

Another major expense would be taxes, for we are
to "render unto Caesar the things that are Caesar's." We
are to "render . . . to all their dues; tribute to whom tribute
is due; custom to whom custom; fear to whom fear" (Romans 13:7).

Naturally, many other expenses arise. The kind and
amount vary with different people. Each individual must
take responsibility for justifying the way he spends his
money.

> Steward I and not possessor of the wealth entrusted me.
> What, were God Himself the holder, would His disposition be?
> This I ask myself each morning, every noon, and every night
> As I view His gentle goodness with an ever new delight.
> —Strickland Gillilan

2. Much money is spent unnecessarily

Suppose our hypothetical salesman, seeing a beautiful
dress he wants his wife to have and a new toy for his
baby, buys them and pays out of his company expense
account. This is an unjustifiable expense.

Christians are not innocent of careless money spending. What was yesterday's luxuries become today's con-
veniences and tomorrow's necessities. Exposed to lavish

display of chrome-plated appliances, the latest gadgets in radio, TV, and hi-fi, and unending counters of attractive merchandise in our shopping centers, people cannot resist buying. The high standard of living demands a high standard of spending. Because our neighbors and friends have some new piece of furniture, photographic equipment, or a swimming pool, we must have it too. Someone has said, "We spend money we don't have, to buy things we don't need, to please people we don't like!"

A magazine article, "Why Nobody Can Save Any More," tells the predicament of a young executive who makes $12,000 a year. Though the average person would consider a salary of $1,000 a month sufficient for any family, the executive worries every week as he figures and refigures the family finances. Monthly expenses which he and his wife seemingly cannot possibly reduce amount to $905. In addition, their frivolities each month include $15 for liquor, $30 for eating out once a week, and $20 for baby-sitters, which then leaves a balance of $30 between the family and financial ruin, with nothing in the budget for saving and next to nothing for insurance. Also, a larger home and second car seemed to be needed soon.

Readers making less than $1,000 per month may find it hard to sympathize with this executive, spotting several places in the detailed budget where expenses could easily be cut down without hardship. The frivolities would come in for drastic revision when so much is spent for eating out and baby-sitters. One trouble is that as our income rises, our expenses soar too. Somehow we shift into a higher bracket of living. Once we climb to a higher level, we never wish to descend to our former status. But honest inspection of our expenses would show several items where reduction is easily possible.

Since we must give an account of ourselves and not of our neighbors, let us not be critical of someone else for having too many clothes, too big a car, or too lavish a house. Let's look into our own expenditures to make sure we can justify each one. One ground of judgment on

Babylon was for luxurious living (Revelation 18:7). Can
we justify our model of car when millions around the
world go to bed hungry each night? Can we spend an extra large amount on a new home when millions are homeless
or living in hovels? Can we indulge freely in so many
expensive luxuries when hundreds of missionary candi-
dates need support to wing them on their way?

A poorly paid faculty member from a Christian college
was visiting in the home of a highly paid executive who
taught a men's Bible class. Getting the only hat he possessed on the way out, the prof quickly counted 17 hats
in the executive's closet. He couldn't help wondering if
every one was needed, since he couldn't wear more than
one at a time!

> I thought of it once as I sat by myself,
> And looked at some boxes that stood on the shelf.
> One was so large, with a contrast so grim,
> A band-box for me, and a mite-box for Him.
>
> I paid for my hat, and I paid for my gown,
> And I paid for the furs that I purchased downtown,
> And when I returned it was plain as could be,
> A mite-box for Him and a band-box for me.
>
> I put in a nickel; it did not seem right.
> I could not be proud of that curious sight.
> So, I took out my check-book and tried to be square,
> For I wanted my giving to look like my prayer.
> —*Author Unknown*

3. *Misusing money is to be guilty of misappropriation of
funds.*

Let us go back to our hypothetical salesman. If he
uses company money to buy furs for his wife, toys or
bicycles for his children, he is virtually embezzling company money and making himself liable for prosecution.
Similarly, the Christian who uses money foolishly, waste-
fully, unnecessarily, unjustifiably, is misappropriating funds
that do not belong to him and leaving himself open for divine condemnation.

A young man appeared on the street with a magnificent

diamond which he had never before worn. Admiring friends exclaimed, "My, that's a beauty! It must have cost a thousand dollars! Where did you get it?"

The proud possessor of the gem replied, "Yes, it cost more than a thousand dollars. It cost $1500. My father gave it to me. It was like this: My father died and in his will he said, 'Here is $1500 for my son, with which he is to erect a stone to my memory!' And fellows," said the young man, pointing to the diamond, "that is the stone!"

Perhaps we have been using the Lord's money to buy useless bubbles with which to decorate our own vain fancies. The Lord wants us to use as much of His wealth as possible to build His kingdom here. But we use it to build our magnificent homes, expensively outfit ourselves, and buy numerous unnecessary things when half the world is without the Gospel. Can we live on an island of luxury in an ocean of poverty?

Before we sit down to enjoy the wonders of heaven, every one of us will be called before the judgment seat for an evaluation of our Christian life. A record of our deeds, words, time spent, and money expended will be scrutinized. John Wesley once observed that some Methodists were twice as rich as when they became Methodists, some four times as rich, and others ten times so. He remarked, "Whilst you get all you can and save all you can, you do not give all you can. Then you are tenfold more the child of hell than you were before."

4. Money left over should go back to the owner

The salesman is expected to return to his company every cent of money over and above his legitimate expenses. Likewise, God wants the Christian to keep for himself only what he justifiably needs, then give back to Him the rest. Perhaps in the long run *a better test of stewardship is not how much we give, but how little we keep for ourselves.*

A man may give $1,000 to the church a year, while a poor lady may give $200. Though the earthly records indicate the man gave five times as much as the lady, the annals of heaven may show that the lady really gave much more because her income was only a fraction of his and she kept far less for her own personal, selfish ends. Paul commended people who gave beyond their ability (II Corinthians 8:3).

In a recent year philanthropic gifts of those filing income tax returns averaged slightly over two percent of their income. The group reporting incomes from $10,000 to $50,000 gave slightly over two percent of their income. The rate for those with incomes under $3,000 was nearly three percent. In reality, those who gave more gave less, and those who gave less really gave more.

Is not this the main thrust of the story of the widow's mite? Because He was vitally interested in our giving, Jesus sat by the treasury, noting how some rich men pompously made a great ado about their gifts. He also spotted a miserably poor widow unostentatiously drop in her offering. He knew all about her, where she lived, her difficult time, that the extent of her assets was two mites, that she was a widow. The word *mite,* the smallest of coins, is a contraction of the Latin *minutum,* which gives the French word *miete,* which means *crumb* or *small morsel.* Some estimate that a mite equaled .17 cents. Two mites would be little more than 1/5 of a cent, so small you probably couldn't hear their clink.

Appraising her gift by heaven's arithmetic, the Lord said that she gave more than all the rich men, for she cast in all she had, whereas they out of their abundance tossed in but a fraction. A church treasurer was giving his annual report. "Mr. A. has given $250." There was a round of applause. "Mr. B. has given $500." Louder applause. "Mr. C. has given $1,000." Tumultuous applause. "Widow D. has given $20." There was silence. In the hush the chairman said, "I think I hear the clapping of the pierced hands."

Many people hide behind the excuse, "Oh, if I only had lots of money, I would give more to the Lord's work."

What we do with the little is exactly what we would do with a lot. If we keep much for ourself with a little income, we would keep much with a big income. An older Christian in Cuba said to a new Christian whose name was Christobel, "If you had 100 sheep, would you give 50 of them for the Lord's work?" "Yes, I would." "Christobel, if you had 100 cows, would you give 50 of them for the Lord's work?" "Yes, I would." "Christobel, would you do the same if you had 100 horses?" "Yes, Teofilo, I would." "Christobel, if you had two pigs, would you give one of them to Him?" "No, I wouldn't," snapped Christobel, "and you have no right to ask me, Teofilo, for you know I have two pigs!"

Incidentally, we should never call a small offering "the widow's mite" unless it is half of one's possession, for a mite was one-half of the widow's two mites. A prosperous merchant was asked for a contribution for a charitable cause. "Yes, I'll give you my mite," he replied. "Do you mean the widow's mite?" asked the collector. Receiving an affirmative answer, the collector exclaimed, "I shall be satisfied with your mite. How much are you worth?" The merchant did some quick arithmetic, "Around $70,000." "Then," said the collector, "give me your check for $35,000. The widow had only two mites, so her 'mite' is half of all she had."

When the poor in the Early Church needed relief, some well-to-do saints sold their land and houses and gave the proceeds to the apostles to distribute to the needy.

Augustine sold the estate which his father left to him and gave the entire proceeds to the poor, reserving nothing for himself. Afterward he gave away more than a tenth of his income and refused to wear expensive garments.

It is related of the sixth-century Gregory that he was so earnest in his concern for the poor that once he grieved for days on hearing that a man had died of starvation in Rome. He accused himself of being his murderer.

John Wesley's famous rule on money says, "Gain all you can. Save all you can. Give all you can." In gaining money, one must do nothing harmful to his neighbor, sell nothing which would impair health, refrain from wrong employments, but engage only in helpful service to his fellow men. Neither was he to save to the point of hazarding the physical or moral health of his dependents or himself. Failure to give all beyond that needed to support one's family, to run one's business, and to provide reasonably for dependents was equal to flouting the command not to lay up treasures on earth. When Wesley's salary was fifty pounds a year, he set aside five pounds for the Lord, a tithe. When his salary had risen to a hundred pounds a year he was still living on forty-five pounds a year and he gave fifty-five pounds to the Lord.

The English statesman, Wilberforce, gave generously to the Lord's work. In 1801, a year of tragic unemployment, his gifts to the poor exceeded his income by 3,000 pounds. He disposed of property, stopped luxuries, lived simply, so that he rarely gave less than a quarter of his income to the poor, besides liberal gifts to other benevolent causes both in England and abroad.

You can live on less when you have more to live for. Motivated by the love of Christ, should not believers somehow be able to cut down on unnecessary expense so they will have more to give to the Lord's work? When one critic of the Christian faith said, "It seems to me that Christianity is one continuous give, give, give," he gave an accurate picture. Our devotion is always costing us something. One objector who decried the repeated requests for gifts to the Lord's work received this answer. "A baby boy was born into our family. He cost us money in doctor's bills and hospital expense. When we brought him home, it cost more money for bottles, crib, baby food, and clothes. As he grew older, he was always costing me something — shirts, socks, food, bicycle, and every few months he needed new shoes. When he went to school, I had to pay for books and lunches. But one day he died, and now he doesn't cost me a cent."

"Giving is living," the angel said,
"Go feed to the hungry sweet charity's bread."
"And must I keep giving and giving again?"
My selfish and querulous answer ran —
"Oh, no," said the angel, his eyes pierced me through,
"Just give till the Master stops giving to you."

"I asked for money, not for food," replied a panhandler as a man offered to take the street beggar into a restaurant. "Of course, I'm hungry. I haven't eaten a good meal in three days," he continued in response to the surprised look on the man's face. "I'm a Communist. We need money for literature!"

In the *Witness*, Whittaker Chambers tells how Alger Hiss and his wife sent Mrs. Hiss' son by a former marriage to college. Mrs. Hiss' first husband paid for it. But they sent him to a cheaper college, so they could use the balance for the Communist party. They also moved into a cheaper house, so they could give more money to the party.

Though Frances R. Havergal wrote the hymn, "Take My Life and Let It Be Consecrated, Lord, to Thee," in 1874, it wasn't till 1878 that the lines were put in print. When she read the verse,

Take my silver and my gold,
Not a mite would I withhold.

she was suddenly convicted of inconsistency. She possessed an unusual collection of fine jewelry, mostly by gift or inheritance, and an unusually lovely jewel box. She packed the jewel box with every piece of jewelry except for half a dozen pieces which were special memorials of her loved ones, and sent it to her church missionary society. She also included a check to cover the value of the jewels she kept. She testifies, "I never packed a box with such pleasure."

On his 25th birthday, the famous ex-cricketer missionary, C. T. Studd, inherited roughly $125,000. Reading the story of the rich young ruler, he gave it all away coolly and deliberately. He sent $25,000 to D. L. Moody which was used to help build Moody Bible Institute's original structure. He gave $25,000 to George Muller for missionary and orphanage work, and another $25,000 to the Salvation Army in India. After a few more gifts, he presented the balance of around $15,000 to his bride for a wedding present. Not to be outdone, she gave every bit of it away to the Lord's work.

Someone has said, "Stewardship is what happens to mine because of what has happened to me." A boy had been just baptized. The minister was personally helping the boy with his clothes after the baptism. From the lad's wet garments fell a little brown wallet. "Is this your purse?" asked the preacher, picking it up off the floor. "Yes, sir," responded the boy. "You see, I wanted my wallet baptized too!"

> The maximum for the Master,
> The minimum for me.
> With ministry to all in need,
> Henceforth my rule shall be.
> To Him who died that I might live
> My time, my means, myself I give.
>
> —*Author Unknown*

Yellow Fever

4

Yellow Fever

Yellow fever is an acute, infectious, often fatal disease characterized, among other symptoms, by jaundice, hemorrhages, and nausea. Transmitted by the mosquito, it occurs in tropical and semi-tropical regions.

Another sickness likewise acute, infectious, and often fatal, though not confined to the tropics, is a fever for that yellow thing called gold. It is caused by a bug called "greed." Yellow fever also goes by the name of money malady or mammon madness.

The grasping man doesn't possess wealth. Wealth possesses him. He has money in the same way an ill man has a fever burning and consuming him, as if molten gold were flowing in his veins. The victim of yellow fever has a flush on his cheek and a glint of steel in his eyes. Someone has called money "the wolf in the breast."

DIAGNOSIS

The main symptom of yellow fever is love of money. Note that it is not *money*, but the *love of money*. Often people mistakenly remark, "Money is the root of all evil." This is false. Correctly quoted, the Bible says, "The *love of money* is the root of all evil" (I Timothy 6:10).

Money itself is neither moral or immoral. It is made good or bad by those who handle it. One may have a right attitude toward it and use it wisely. Or one may have a wrong attitude toward it and misuse it. An inordinate affection for money is a wrong attitude and leads to many evils. In Shakespeare's *Romeo and Juliet*, after Romeo

65

bribes an apothecary to sell him some poison (which was against the law) Romeo says, while paying,

> There's thy gold, worse poison to men's souls,
> Doing more murders, in this loathsome world,
> Than these poor compounds that thou mayest not sell.
> I sell thee poison; thou hast sold me none.

Yet money is not always poison causing death. It may be a potion giving life. Money feeds and clothes families, sends young people to college, buys medicine for the sick, purchases books, builds churches, dispatches missionaries, and helps the poor. Not all lucre is filthy. A barber in New York state was handed $300 in $20 bills to keep in a safe place. He put the money in his wallet, then wrapped it in a towel. When the laundry picked up the family linen, the wallet went along with it. Detectives found the wallet and money, intact but damp, whirling around in one of the firm's washing machines. It was clean! Money can drive men to paradise or drown them in perdition.

How wonderful when the Lord gets possession of rich men. The pulpit need not talk money down. Power to get wealth is from the Lord (Deuteronomy 8:18). The Lord Jesus never taught that devotion to business necessarily hindered spiritual life. To the Christian all of life is sacred, with no division into spiritual and secular segments. Making money at a trade is as sacred as doing missionary work in Thailand. An auto mechanic working on an old motor in a garage pit was asked by a passerby, "What are you doing?" "I'm preaching the Gospel to the lands beyond the sea," he replied as he kept on tinkering, his mechanical ability consecrated to God. The ring of his tools was as sweet in divine ears as the eloquence of a preacher. God can be served by diligent business men out to make money for God's kingdom. To undervalue money is as wrong as to overvalue it. Laziness which results in poverty doesn't please the Lord who uttered the parable of the talents. Money-making for the Lord's glory becomes holy service to God.

The tragedy is that men become enamored of mammon. They want more and more until they become money-mad. In 1848, "yellow fever" broke out like a plague all over the civilized world. The magic word "gold" which had excited men for centuries propelled people from everywhere toward California, though California was then hardly more than a name. But with the cry, "There's gold in them thar' hills," the rush began. Eager seekers of fortune abandoned comfortable homes and lucrative jobs to escape boredom. Poorly equipped for the dangerous journey, they were unprepared for the hazards of the road. The gold they knew about; but no one told them of the hardships. So the caravans rolled on and on with brave spirits singing to the tune of "O Susannah":

> I soon shall be in Frisco
> And then I'll look around,
> And when I see the gold lumps there,
> I'll pick them off the ground.
> O California,
> That's the land for me;
> I'm bound for San Francisco
> With a washbowl on my knee.

Canvas-covered schooners plus wagons of every description struggled across prairie and desert. Many came to a halt as the exhausted horses died, leaving the travelers in despair. Though groups banded together for protection at night, Indian attacks often ended their search for gold. Cholera and other diseases killed many. Frequently sufferers were left to die while their panic-stricken companions pushed on. Herds of buffalo stampeded some caravans. Lack of water thinned out the ranks of others, especially on the southern route through parched areas. The trail from Fort Leavenworth, customary starting place, to Fort Laramie at the foot of the Rockies was strewn with broken wagons, abandoned equipment and clearly marked graves of men, women, and children. Though every disaster known to the West struck time and time again, crowds continued to pour into California. Ships of seven seas sailed into

San Francisco harbor, battered by storm on the rough passage around Cape Horn. Often the crews disembarked with the passengers, totally deserting their ship, leaving the captain alone on his vessel swaying idly at anchor. Thousands found their way to California by way of the Isthmus of Panama, but other thousands were taken by tropical disease and heat prostration. San Francisco, which previously had but fifty dwellings, mushroomed into a sea of tents and shacks covering hills from top to bottom. Food prices skyrocketed to fabulous values, with eggs $1 each. Lumber which sold at $100 in New York cost $1,400 there. Brawls, vice, gambling, drunkenness, robbery, and murder erupted on every hand. Many of our TV Westerns reflect the lawlessness of that period which was the concomitant of yellow fever. "Mammon led them on."

Love of money is nothing more or less than covetousness. The verse, "Let your conversation be without covetousness" (Hebrews 13:5), is translated in the Revised Version, "Be ye free from the love of money." "Without covetousness" in the original language is but one word with three parts: *No — love of — money.* Covetousness is an excessive desire for something. Since most "somethings" can be secured through the medium of money, covetousness and love of money boil down to the same sin.

Mammon originally meant that in which men were apt to confide. Because so many trusted in money, mammon came to mean riches, wealth, money. Covetousness is a form of idolatry. We wouldn't be so grossly ignorant as to bow down to gods of wood and stone, yet we worship at the shrine of the almighty dollar sign. This refined form of image worship is rebuked by the very last verse in the apostle John's first epistle, "Little children, keep yourselves from idols. Amen" (I John 5:21).

Covetousness is listed with the worst of sins in several New Testament passages. "But now I have written unto you not to keep company, if any man that is called a brother be a fornicator, or *covetous,* or an idolater, or a railer, or a drunkard, or an extortioner" (I Corinthians 5:11). "But fornication, and all uncleanness, or *covetousness,* let it not be once named among you, as becometh saints" (Ephesians 5:3). In another epistle, *covetousness* is mentioned in the same breath as fornication, uncleanness, anger, wrath, malice, blasphemy, filthy communication, and lying (Colossians 3:5-9). In this same passage covetousness is plainly called idolatry. When our Lord named the sins which proceeded out of the heart of men, he placed *covetousness* in the middle of evil thoughts, adulteries, fornications, murders, thefts, and wickedness, deceit, lasciviousness, an evil eye, blasphemy, pride, foolishness (Mark 7:21-23). When Paul lists the characteristics of the last perilous days, he heads up the catalog thus, "For men shall be lovers of their own selves, *covetous.*" Instead of centering his life in God, man will concentrate on himself, resulting in covetousness for his own self-centered kingdom.

No place is too sacred, no sphere too lofty, for covetousness to attempt to intrude. No enterprise is too venturesome. Heaven itself was the scene of its first occurrence when Lucifer coveted God's position. Says the poet Milton, in personifying cupidity,

> For even in heaven his looks and thoughts
> Were always downward bent; admiring more
> The riches of heaven's pavement, trodden gold,
> Than aught divine or holy else, enjoyed
> In vision beatific.

The initial sin of the Bible involved covetousness. Eve desired the forbidden fruit. Her iniquity resulted in the fall of mankind. The very first recorded transgression of the Early Church included covetousness. Ananias and Sapphira coveted part of the sale price of their property and withheld it for themselves while pretending to give the total proceeds. Covetousness advertises itself all over the pages of both Old and New Testaments. Significantly, every time the term "filthy lucre" occurs in the New Testament, it has reference to church officers or teachers, showing the lurking danger of covetousness infiltrating the motives of spiritual leaders. Because covetousness is a sin of the spirit

invisible to other eyes (though its consequences may later
be strikingly revealed in a physical way), covetousness
can be indulged in during church services, inordinately
wanting this, immoderately desiring that, even while the
choir is singing or the preacher speaking.

Covetousness is a deceptive sin. No one thinks he is
covetous. It parades under specious names like economy,
foresight, and prudence. Where does wise saving end and
greed begin? At what point does a man cease to save for his
family and cross over into the quest for riches? There is
such a point, which is to be determined by the individual
conscience. But how easy it is for our selfish minds to
rationalize our covetousness! A confessor to many peni-
tents said, "No one ever confessed covetousness." One
minister stated, "Among all the prayers in prayer meeting
and deep confessions of sin in times of searching, I have
never once heard the sin of covetousness confessed." One
preacher spoke on this vice under the subject, "The Sin
We Are Afraid to Mention." So universal, so hidden, so
powerful, but so deceptive is it that we are scarcely aware
of its existence.

In evaluating the various commandments in the Decalogue, many people would minimize the importance of the
tenth which reads, "Thou shalt not covet." Compared to
murder, adultery, and theft, how unimportant it sounds!
But this command is crucial on several grounds. For one
reason, this particular precept enters the arena of thought
life and demands conformity to the will of God in our in-
ner being. The other commands stated demand overt obedience. This one penetrates beyond outer behavior and
pierces into our thoughts, intents, and motives, which are
unseen to men but known to God. It was this specific command that brought conviction of sin to Paul who lived an
otherwise outwardly holy life (Romans 7:7-10).

Another factor that makes this command significant
is that victory here will make for victory in areas covered
by the other commands. But covetousness unchecked leads
into almost every type of known sin. Coveting someone's

reputation may lead to slander, false witness, and lying. Coveting another's wealth leads to theft or dishonesty. Coveting someone's wife leads to adultery. Coveting something badly enough may lead to murder. The commonest form of covetousness is love of money which leads to a host of iniquities. No wonder Jesus said, "Beware of covetousness" (Luke 12:15).

PROGNOSIS

Unless checked, yellow fever can develop serious complications. "The love of money is the parent of all sin." Money malady may lead to the following ills:

1. *Stealing*

When Mary anointed Jesus not long before His death, Judas Iscariot objected on the grounds that the ointment should have been sold and the proceeds given to the poor. However, the sacred writer gives us Judas' real reason. He was a thief and in charge of the money in the bag (the disciples' funds). His covetousness which had led him to steal on previous occasions saw another golden opportunity to confiscate some money evade his grasp. Yellow fever made one of the Twelve a thief (John 12:5, 6). Love of money is the major cause of bank robberies, thefts, burglaries, juggling of accounts, pilfering of cash, and absconding with funds.

Though the Lord had distinctly ordered the Israelites not to take any booty from the captured city of Jericho, Achan couldn't resist his love of money. "When I saw among the spoils a goodly Babylonish garment, and two hundred shekels of silver, and a wedge of gold of fifty shekels weight, then I coveted them, and took them" (Joshua 7:21). The result was temporary defeat of Israel at the hands of Ai, the loss of 36 lives, and later exposure and death for Achan and his family. After a tornado leveled several blocks in Flint, Michigan, a few years ago, three out-of-town policemen were arrested for looting.

When we fail to tithe, we rob God (Malachi 3:8, 9). Why do people neglect to give this portion to the Lord's work? Honest confession would in most cases reveal that people don't wish to part with their money because they prize it too highly. They are victims of yellow fever.

2. Gambling

Gambling, a form of stealing, takes from another without returning equal value. It makes one richer at the expense of another. The root motive for gambling is mammon madness.

Most get-rich-schemes are gambles. In addition, they are likely to be tinged with dishonesty. "He that maketh haste to be rich shall not be innocent" (Proverbs 28:20). A Greek line says, "No righteous man e'er grew rich suddenly." A Spanish proverb reads, "Who would be rich in a year gets hanged in half a year." An Italian saying has it, "The river does not become swollen with clear water." The search for easy money is spurred by too intense a desire for money.

3. Debt

A generation ago people saved in advance to purchase things with cash. Today we buy on credit. Though on occasion borrowing may be necessary and buying on time advisable, yellow fever always carries the possibility of sinking a person inextricably in debt. "The borrower is servant to the lender" (Proverbs 22:7). Someone has said, "He that goes a-borrowing goes a-sorrowing." An old saying goes like this:

Rags make paper.
Paper makes money.
Money makes banks.
Banks make loans.
Loans make poverty.
Poverty makes rags.

4. Lying

When Naaman, captain of the Syrian hosts, was cleansed of his leprosy through the ministry of Elisha, he wanted to give the prophet a financial reward, but Elisha firmly but politely refused. However, Elisha's servant, Gehazi, a victim of yellow fever, pursued after Naaman, pretended his master had changed his mind and asked for a talent of silver and two changes of garments. Naaman gave him double his request. But God revealed to Elisha his servant's greed and he pronounced the punishment of leprosy on Gehazi and his family forever (II Kings 5:15-27). "Ill gotten gain brings ruin in its train."

5. *Bribery*

On a mission field in Southern Rhodesia the police were asked why they persecuted and imprisoned the Christians. It was pointed out to the police that whereas these Christians formerly stole, lied, and committed crimes, they were now law-abiding citizens. The police responded, "Don't you know that if all these people turned to the Jesus way we wouldn't have any jobs? These Christians won't pay us any bribes."

Old Testament prophets often spoke out against judges who could be bought off. "The heads thereof judge for reward" (Micah 3:11). Even Samuel's sons were guilty of bribery (I Samuel 8:3). The Roman soldiers at Jesus' tomb were given a large sum of money to deny the Resurrection and to say that Jesus' disciples came and stole His body away while they slept (Matthew 28:11-15). Because he hoped to receive money to release Paul from prison, Felix kept him bound for two years (Acts 24:26). Sports fans are often shocked when they learn that well-known players have betrayed their team and deliberately "thrown" the game for money.

One judge, whose rough-and-ready brand of justice was certainly drastic, though not exemplary, began a case by saying, "I have $10,000 in one pocket given me by the plaintiff to judge the case in his favor. I have $15,000 in my other pocket given me by the defendant to tip the scales in his direction. I shall return $5,000 to the defendant and judge the case on its merits!"

6. Cheating

Scandals of recent years involving short-weights by butchers, thesis preparation by ghost writers, and TV quiz fixes all point up the sad truth that love of money makes people cheat.

Charles Van Doren in official testimony before the Congressional investigating committee admitted that his wish to win money led him to apply as a contestant for a quiz program. He tells how before his first appearance on "Twenty-one" he was visited by a producer who informed him that it was standard procedure to tip off contestants with the answers and that the current winner on the program had to be defeated in order to increase the entertainment value of the program. (Greater value would mean more listeners, which would mean more buyers of products, which would mean more profits for the sponsors, which would mean more money to love.) Van Doren hesitated but was guaranteed $1,000 to appear for one night. He recalled, "I will not describe to this committee the intense moral struggle that went on inside me. I was sick at heart. Yet the fact is that I unfortunately agreed, after some time, to his proposal." After that first program on which he tied the other contestant three times, Van Doren was told he would win the next week and be the new champion. His guarantee was increased to $8,000. One episode of cheating led to another, as he was coached on how to answer the questions, pausing before some, skipping certain parts and returning to them, hesitating and building up suspense. Someone put it, "Little white lies soon became double features in technicolor," all for the love of money. "He that is greedy of gain troubleth his own house; but he that hateth gifts shall live" (Proverbs 15:27).

7. Oppression

Most rich farm land in England was once owned by lords. Despite the scarcity of money, rent was usually charged in terms of silver. Collecting agents like the notorious Captain Boycott were merciless in their abuse of tenants. If a farmer could not produce enough silver to pay the rent, collectors would often drive their wagons right into the field as the wheat was being cut and force the farmer to settle in grain at a price well below market. Farmers gritted their teeth when ordered to literally fork over their choice produce. This practice of "forking over" has come to stand for any enforced relinquishment of property or money.

Laban oppressed Jacob by making him work seven more years for the right to marry Rachel. Altogether Laban changed Jacob's wages ten times, undoubtedly to the disadvantage of Jacob. The person who refuses to sell corn during a famine when people are hungry, waiting for prices to go higher, shall bring a curse on his own head; but he that selleth shall be blessed (Proverbs 11:26). "He that oppresseth the poor to increase his riches . . . shall surely come to want" (Proverbs 22:16). Sometimes men become rich by violence, running rough-shod over the downtrodden in the pursuit of gold (Micah 6:12). Shady business practices, excessive pricing and ruthless monopolies can grind under the less fortunate. A man may steal from a railroad car and go to jail for a year, but some financier may steal the whole railroad under the guise of shrewd business.

The Lord hears the cries of slave laborers whose wages have been withheld or reduced because of the greed of the rich (James 5:4).

8. *Family-breakdown*

Someone has said, "Troubles in marriage often begin when a man becomes so busy earning his salt that he forgets his sugar." A man's love of money may make him neglect his wife and family. Or love of money may lead both husbands and wives to extravagance and financial troubles. High on the list of causes of divorce is incompatibility, perhaps better spelled "*income*-patibility." Eighty dollars per week income with seventy-nine dollars weekly expenses may keep the marriage delightful, but eighty dollars income with eighty-one dollars expenses may make it disastrous.

Knowing a man had plenty has led many a woman to set her feather for that man, even though he was married. It has been said, "Cold cash has been known to warm many a woman's heart." Gold diggers have broken up many marriages or led men into ridiculous alliances.

Yellow fever has caused bad feelings between brothers and sisters. A man called out to Jesus one day, "Master, speak to my brother, that he divide the inheritance with me" (Luke 12:13). Our Lord's answer was a warning against covetousness. Someone has said, "Where there's a will, there's a relative or a lawsuit." A father left his estate equally between two married daughters. One had borrowed heavily from her father and owed his estate a large sum, half of which her sister could have rightfully claimed. But she declined to make an issue over it, kept silence, was cheated out of a fair amount, but remained good friends with her sister. She didn't let love of money destroy her relationship with her sister.

9. Wrong kind of business

The owners of the demon-possessed girl in Philippi were angry when she was healed through Paul's ministry, because their source of revenue was gone. They cared more about money than about seeing the soothsayer in her right mind (Acts 16:16-21).

Money madness sent the silversmiths of Ephesus into an uproar over Paul's preaching, because his message showed the futility and error of idolatry, with the resultant drop in sale of their Diana shrines (Acts 20:23-27).

The president of a religious publishing company stated that at a meeting of publishers of secular books they frankly admitted that the reason they published rotten fiction was to pay the bills. Because they didn't earn enough profit on good types, they had to make money on filthy literature. Said one publisher, "I wouldn't dare take the books I accept for publication home for my family to read!" A writer walked into a publisher's office, plunked down a manuscript on his desk and exclaimed, "There it is! Print it just as it is. Don't put a blue line through any of it. I know it's dirty, but you need the money and so do I." Another publisher said, "There are two important events in life, birth and death. From now on all books we publish will deal with rape and murder!"

10. Breakdown of the Lord's Day

Nehemiah had to rebuke the Israelites in the days of the restoration for bringing goods into Jerusalem on the sabbath to sell (Nehemiah 13:15-22).

A theater in a Pennsylvania town where Sunday movies were prohibited hung out a motto, "Go to church Sunday; attend movies during the week." But when a referendum to permit Sunday movies was proposed, the theater scrapped its motto and worked hard for an affirmative vote. Sunday opening meant more shekels.

11. Murder

Judas' yellow fever not only led him to pilfer from the treasurer's bag, but to finally sell Jesus to certain death for a paltry thirty pieces of silver. Ahasuerus, king of Persia, was willing to let wicked Haman slay thousands of Jews in return for a payment of 10,000 talents of silver into his treasury.

A few years ago a plane took off from Quebec City airport, then crashed a few minutes later, killing 23 people, among them a Mrs. Guay. Police accused Mr. Guay of placing a time bomb on the plane to collect a $10,000 insurance policy. The man who made the homemade bomb for Guay did it for the pittance price of a $10 ring. He claimed he didn't know the real purpose of the bomb, but though crippled, he had hobbled to a vantage point on the terrace of the Chateau-Frontenac Hotel to watch the ill-fated plane fly out of Quebec City. Mammon often leads to murder.

12. War

Munitions makers have been charged with fomenting war to make profits, even with selling arms to both sides in a conflict. The real cause of war is the desire to improve economic status and make possible a higher standard of living. Territorial aggrandizement, colonial expansion, and capture of areas with valuable resources like oil all stem from money malady (James 4:1, 2). Once when Frederick the Great of Prussia wished to annex some adjoining territory he asked his Minister of War to write out a proclamation of war. He began it, "Whereas in the providence of God — " "Stop that lying," thundered Frederick. "Just say, 'Frederick wants more land.' "

13. Muddling the motives of religious workers

When Balak asked the prophet Balaam to prophesy against Israel, Balaam persisted in trying to give a message that would please Balak. The New Testament states the reason clearly. Balaam loved the *wages* of unrighteousness (II Peter 2:15).

Some men have entered the ministry for the money in it. A few evangelists have commercialized their campaigns. Remember that every time the expression "filthy lucre" occurs in the New Testament, it is in connection with church leaders or religious teachers. One qualification for a bishop is that he must be "not greedy of filthy lucre" (I Timothy 3:3), or "not given to filthy lucre" (Titus 1:7).

Elders are to feed the flock of God, "not for filthy lucre, but of a ready mind" (I Peter 5:2). The same demand is put upon the deacon (I Timothy 3:8). False teachers are described as those deceivers who teach "things which they ought not, for filthy lucre's sake" (Titus 1:11). Peter says of false prophets, "Through covetousness shall they with feigned words make merchandise of you" (II Peter 2:3). Yellow fever can enter into the motives of those who profess to speak for God to men, shading off the message, toning down the truth, for the sake of scratching the ears of those whose offerings furnish their livelihood.

14. *Perdition*

To catch monkeys, some Africans take a big pumpkin from their garden, cut a hole in the middle just big enough for a monkey to put his hand in. After scraping out the pumpkin seeds, the African half-fills the pumpkin with corn which the monkey likes. Along comes Mr. Monkey who puts his hand in to take as much corn as he can hold. Then the poor monkey can't get his hand out. He pulls and pulls but in vain. If he would only let go of some of the corn, he could get his hand out. But Mr. Monkey is too greedy to do that. Soon the African sees that the monkey is caught, runs from his hiding place, grabs his club, and heads straight for the monkey. Mr. Monkey sees him coming with the big club, knows that the African is no friend of his and that the club will kill him. In spite of all this, he will not let go of the corn. Instead, he just scolds and chatters at the man till the man ends it all with his club and the monkey has no need of any more corn.

Enamored of money, there are people who would rather grasp on to their little world of wealth and lose their own soul. Rich men fared poorly in Jesus' parables and teachings. Covetousness can neutralize the effect of the preaching of the Gospel, like the seed that was choked by the "deceitfulness of riches." One man never heard a word of most sermons because he was thinking about his thriving business. He had more business than he had any business to have. Jesus said it was easier for a camel to go through the eye of a needle than for a rich man to enter the kingdom of heaven. Love of money prevented the rich young ruler from following Jesus. Love of money helped put Dives and the rich fool in hell.

A penny can blot out the sun if held close enough to the eye. Money can eclipse the Sun of righteousness. Paul puts it strongly, "They that will be rich fall into temptation and a snare, and into many foolish and hurtful lusts, which drown men in destruction and perdition" (I Timothy 6:9). Just as a woman was burned to death in her flaming home when she went back inside to retrieve $10 in her purse, so people may find themselves in a lost eternity because they were so preoccupied with the tinsel and coins of this godless world system.

In his inimitable allegory, *Pilgrim's Progress,* John Bunyan describes how professing pilgrims, Hold-the-world, Money-love, and Save-all, leave the road at the suggestion of Demas to look at a silver mine in a little hill called *Lucre.* He comments, "Whether they fell into the pit by looking over the brink thereof, or whether they went down to dig, or whether they were smothered in the bottom by the damps that commonly arise, of these things I am not certain; but this I observed, that they never were seen again in the way."

CURE

Hippocrates, the famous Greek physician for whom the Hippocratic oath which doctors take is named, once proposed a consultation of all the physicians in the world to find a cure for covetousness. Since man is inherently selfish, he needs a transformation of his moral nature, which can be effected by the new birth or regeneration. With the life of Christ indwelling him, he possesses new power which can enable him to be giving instead of greedy, sacrificial instead of selfish, and generous instead of grasping.

Someone has advised, "If you wish to be delivered from the love of money, give freely." First of all, we should give our tithe to the Lord's work. Then we should consider the balance as belonging to the Lord to be given back to Him after essential expenses are paid. Every opportunity to give should be seized up. The truth of learning experimentally that it is more blessed to give than to receive will help confirm the habit of giving and repulse the tendency to grab. The death of covetousness comes through the birth of charity. The love of Christ for us will elicit the response of our love to Christ so that we shall love God and our neighbor with our money. The man so controlled by the love of money that he stole is commanded to steal no more, but rather to labor with his own hands so that he will be able to give to the needy (Ephesians 4:28).

Contentment rather than covetousness must become the tenor of our life. Our attitudes must be without love of silver (Hebrews 13:5). Paul, who coveted no man's silver, or gold, or apparel, exemplified the life that is not covetous, but charitable (Acts 20:33). We can learn from the frugal farmer who, when visiting a new shopping center for the first time, was asked what he thought of it. He replied, "I don't know when I've seen so many things I could do without."

Two brothers owned a profitable and successful business. Offered a controlling interest in a new company if they would take over and expand it, they refused on the following grounds: "We are men with families. We are also deacons in our church. We are making more than a comfortable living with time left over to forget our business and give our evenings to our families and our church. If we take over this new company, it would mean longer hours with no time for our church or our children. We have decided that we cannot sacrifice our families, our health, and the Lord's work to make more money we really don't need."

"Godliness with contentment is great gain" (I Timothy 6:6), worth more than all the money in the world, and it is the remedy for yellow fever.

Don't Give Till It Hurts

5

Don't Give Till It Hurts

The late Dr. John Broadus, well-known preacher and seminary professor who authored the classic on homiletics, *Preparation and Delivery of Sermons,* left the pulpit one Sunday morning at offering time. Walking over to an usher, he looked over his shoulder and watched every penny, nickel, and dime which the people on the first row gave. Then he followed the usher all the way down the aisle as he moved from row to row, noting what each person dropped into the plate. Some were surprised, some embarrassed, others mad, and a few delighted. Back in the pulpit, Dr. Broadus urged the congregation to forget that he had seen what each gave, but to remember that the sleepless eye of God always watches every gift placed in the collection by His people.

God's eye must behold many strange sights when the offering plate moves through church pews. Americans traveling in Canada are accustomed to having their bills discounted because Canadian money has a higher value. But when suddenly in 1960 American *coins* also became unacceptable unless discounted, Yankee silver began to turn up in abundance in parking meters, vending machines, and church collection plates. One New York church treasurer counting the offering said, "We've a well-traveled congregation today—10 shillings, 5 francs, 2 pesos, a subway token, and a bus transfer!"

When a special offering was taken for work in the Kentucky mountains, a prankster dropped a button on the plate. Later the preacher announced, "Some put dollars in; some put quarters; some put dimes; some put nickels, some put cents; and those who had no sense put buttons!"

Ushers, treasurers, and counting committees may see many "unusual" gifts, but the divine eye sees far more — motive, attitude, frequency, proportion, and sacrifice, if any. These intangibles, fully known to the Omniscient, determine the measure of acceptability of a gift. The Scriptures suggest certain criteria, which if followed will make our offerings pleasing to God.

GIVING SHOULD BE REGULAR AND PROPORTIONATE

Giving is an integral part of the Christian life. God so loved that He gave His only begotten Son. Nor did God stop giving with His supreme gift, but with Him He has continued to freely give us all things. Elizabeth Barrett Browning ends a poem in "Sonnets from the Portuguese" with this line: "God's gifts put man's best dreams to shame." Awareness of God's love-giving should awaken in us the desire to give back to Him and keep on giving.

When a young fellow falls in love, he brings gifts to his girl friend — candy, flowers, and ultimately a ring. When we love the Lord, we will want to give of our material substance to Him. Worship demands giving. Only a few paragraphs past the opening words of Genesis tells of offerings brought by Cain and Abel. The Israelites brought gifts at the three main feasts each year, for the divine command read, "None shall appear before me empty." When Solomon dedicated the temple, he presented 22,000 oxen and 120,000 sheep. The Wise Men brought gifts to the Christ-child. Some early disciples voluntarily sold their houses and lands, giving the proceeds to profit the poor. Pentecost affected property. You can't have genuine, Spirit-filled living without the loosening of purse strings. When the Lord opens our heart, then we should open our purse. Generosity to the Lord's work is economic evidence that we have been redeemed. It has been said, "You can give without loving, but you can't love without giving." The psalmist put it, "Bring an offering and come into his courts" (Psalm 96:8).

Because the "giving" nature of Christianity is not readily grasped by all, many folks avoid offerings or give very little. One preacher remarked, "When I look at my well-dressed congregation, I ask, 'Where are the poor?' When I look at the offering plates, I ask, 'Where are the rich?'" Another commented, "The poor are always welcome in this church, and when I glance at the collection plate I know they have come."

An unemployed preacher with a good physical build wanted to join the police force. The police commissioner interviewed him, expressed gratification at his physical condition, then asked some routine questions, among them, "What would you do to break up a rioting mob?" The minister thought a minute, then answered, "I'd take up a collection!"

Not only should Christians give, but our giving should be regular and proportionate. Paul told the Corinthians, "Now concerning the collection for the saints, as I have given order to the churches of Galatia, even so do ye. Upon the first day of the week let every one of you lay by him in store, as God hath prospered him, that there be no gatherings when I come" (I Corinthians 16:1, 2). Though Paul refers to a particular collection for the poor saints at Jerusalem which he wished taken before he came so that he would not have to take a special offering after his arrival, certain definite principles of giving are plainly presented.

First, every one is to give, whether rich or poor. Second, offerings are to be made on the first day of the week. Since it is rather difficult to take up an offering unless the saints are gathered in a church service, this command is tacit proof that the Christians were meeting for worship on the first day of the week, Sunday, not Saturday. How logical to give an offering on the first day of the week for Sunday commemorates the resurrection of Christ from the grave! Out of gratitude for His victory which makes possible the forgiveness of our sins and the radiant prospect of a raised body like unto Christ's glorious one, we should gladly bring a gift on the anniversary of this event, which is the first day of the week. Thus a real connection exists between the 15th chapter of I Corinthians which deals with the Resurrection theme, and the 16th chapter which begins, "Now concerning the collection. . . ."

Third, gifts are to be regular, not sporadic. It is so easy to fall into the habit of hit-and-miss giving. We tell ourselves we will give later when we are better fixed financially. Or we falsely assume that we are giving more than we do. Spotty, unsystematic giving has a way of appearing far greater than it is. The actual total would be shockingly low if an accurate record were kept by those who generously drop a bill on the plate now and again.

The secretary of the treasury in the reign of France's King Louis XIV was a stingy politician named Etienne de Silhouette who did not enjoy spending public funds, much less his own. For his own mansion he bought the poorest of furniture and shoddiest carpets. On his wall, instead of the usual expensive oil paintings, he hung cheap, outline portraits. With the people of Paris everywhere talking about his smallness, it isn't surprising his black outline portraits were called *silhouettes*. Each week should see us setting aside money for the Lord's work. Otherwise our gifts may be but shadows of what they should be. To those who give now and again, their gifts may show that they are covetous most of the time. In their case, covetousness may be a habit and benevolence but a momentary suspension of covetousness. Of them it could not be said, "You have regularly given," but rather, "You have regularly withheld."

Fourth, giving is to be proportionate — "as God hath prospered." This percentage would be understood to be a minimum of ten percent, because their tutor, Paul, was a Jew and would have taught them tithing. A mother thought it wise to read to her little boy what the Bible said about a tenth, in order to stir up his conscience on the subject. After she had read several passages he asked, "Whom did God say those things to?" "To the Jew," replied his mother. The little lad had picked up a little anti-Semitism through some unwholesome playmates. After thinking a moment, he summed up the whole case for tithing from which there seemed no escape, "Well, I think we ought to give as much as the old Jews anyhow."

GIVING SHOULD BE SINCERE AND FROM THE HEART

A sixteen-year-old girl ran away from home and lived a wayward life. Though on Father's Day, Christmas, and his birthday she sent her father gifts, these presents meant virtually nothing to her broken-hearted dad. He far preferred her living a decent life and sending no presents than sending the most valuable gifts when her life pained him deeply.

Before King Saul went to battle the Amalekites, he was divinely ordered to destroy all the sheep and oxen of the captured people. When he returned from the battle with the best of the sheep and oxen, he was met by Samuel who rebuked him for his disobedience. Saul tried to excuse his insubordination by saying he intended to give these animals to the Lord as a sacrifice. Samuel replied with a truth apropos for giving in all ages, "Hath the Lord as great delight in burnt offerings and sacrifices, as in obeying the voice of the Lord? Behold, to obey is better than sacrifice, and to hearken than the fat of rams" (I Samuel 15:22). God would rather not have our gifts if we are living in rebellion against His Word. The man who deliberately disobeys God and then brings an offering will find that the Lord doesn't want his money. To please God, our gifts must be backed by sincerity of heart.

Money given to the Lord must be earned in an honest way. Ill-gotten gain, such as the fee of a harlot, is not welcome in the church. "Thou shalt not bring the hire of a whore . . . into the house of the Lord thy God" (Deuteronomy 23:18).

"The sacrifice of the wicked is an abomination to the Lord" (Proverbs 15:8). The prophet Isaiah warned of God's dislike for offerings from rebellious people. "To what

purpose is the multitude of your sacrifices unto me? said
the Lord: I am full of the burnt offerings of rams, and
the fat of fed beasts; and I delight not in the blood of
bullocks, or of lambs, or of he-goats" (Isaiah 1:11). The
Lord wanted them to repent and be forgiven first. "Wash
you, make you clean; put away the evil of your doings from
before mine eyes; cease to do evil" (Isaiah 1:16). The sacrifices the Lord wants first of all "are a broken spirit; a
broken and a contrite heart, O God, thou wilt not despise"
(Psalm 51:17). The prophet Jeremiah makes the same point
in giving God's message to lawless people, "To what purpose cometh there to me incense from Sheba, and the
sweet cane from a far country? your burnt offerings are
not acceptable, nor your sacrifices sweet unto me" (Jeremiah 6:20).

Our Lord is more interested in us than in our money.
Paul commended the Corinthians who "first gave their own
selves to the Lord" (II Corinthians 8:5). Unless we first
present our bodies a living sacrifice to the Lord, our money
gifts will be dead and unacceptable sacrifice. Some churches
specifically invite only believers to support their work financially. An announcement at offering time by the pastor will
sound like this, "God's work should be supported by God's
people. If you have been born again into God's family,
we invite you to give. If you are not a believer in the Lord
Jesus Christ, we are not asking you to support His work."

Two contractors were discussing income tax problems.
One contractor, learning that the other gave a sizable chunk
to his church and claimed twenty percent deduction on
his tax return, exclaimed, "Say, you get out of paying a
lot of taxes that way. I'm going to join your church."
The first contractor leaned forward confidentially, "My
friend, I'm afraid you've got the wrong idea about this
thing. You just can't go down and join a church because
you figure it will be a way of dodging part of your tax."
Quite abashed, the reluctant taxpayer roared, "You mean
to tell me your church wouldn't accept me if I came down
there and gave them $20,000 a year? What kind of stuff

are you handing me?" The contractor quietly informed him that he knew many churches that wouldn't accept him unless he were a truly converted man.

You can't deposit money in a bank until you open an account. Nor can you bring money to the bank of heaven until you open your account with the Lord. When you give yourself to the Lord, He opens an account for you.

Christians shouldn't give money to escape responsibility in the Lord's work. For example, paying to missions will not excuse us from praying for missions. Making a $100 gift to the Sunday school to buy off our duty of teaching a class will render the gift invalid.

If in contemplating an offering for the Lord's work, a person remembers that he has wronged a fellow Christian, the Scriptures advise, "Leave there thy gift before the altar, and go thy way; first be reconciled to thy brother, and then come and offer thy gift" (Matthew 5:24). Some things are more important than contributing to the church.

Whatever gift we make to God or man must come from a heart of love. Otherwise, "though I bestow all my goods to feed the poor, . . . and have not charity, it profiteth . . . nothing" (I Corinthians 13:3).

Giving Should Be Willing and Cheerful

At a service on the island of Jamaica held for the purpose of taking a missionary offering, a chairman was elected and the following resolutions adopted. (1) Resolved, that we will all give. (2) Resolved, that we will give as the Lord has prospered us. (3) Resolved, that we will give cheerfully. It was local practice for each person to walk individually to the communion table and deposit his gift under the eye of the presiding officer. One well-to-do member delayed until he was painfully noticeable. When he finally came forward to deposit his gift, the presiding officer said, "That is according to the first resolution, but not according to the second." The member returned indignantly to his seat, taking back his money. But either conscience within or pressure without kept working until he came forward again, doubling his contribution and muttering, "Take that, then." The presiding officer commented, "That may meet the first and second resolutions, but it isn't according to the third." Again the giver retired to his seat. A few minutes later, accepting the rebuke, he came up the third time with a still larger gift and a good-natured smile. Then the chairman exclaimed, "That's according to all resolutions!"

The thought of an offering pains many people. During a revival meeting a man was so stirred by the message that he began to shout loudly, "Praise the Lord! Amen! That's right, brother!" Every few moments he repeated some ejaculations until he became an annoyance with his loud shouting. The preacher realizing this disturbance could not be allowed much longer and knowing that the offender was a man well-known in the community for his stinginess, paused for a moment till he had perfect attention, then quietly said, "Somehow I feel led to stop and take a missionary offering right now. I'd like to invite all of you folks who love the Lord and who like to express your love for Him to give generously." The shouting stopped, the man reached for his hat and quietly slipped out of the meeting.

A southern preacher, fired up both by his subject and by the enthusiasm of his congregation, exclaimed, "Brethren, the church ought to stop walking and get up and run." "Amen," was the rousing response. Encouraged, he continued, "Brethren, the church ought to rise and fly." "Amen," chorused the hearers. "But, brethren," the preacher paused so they would get the full effect, "it will take money to make the church run; it will take finances to make the church fly." Frigid silence followed. Then someone muttered, "Let the church walk."

Giving money to the Lord's work must have caused sorrow to people in Paul's day, for he told the Corinthians to give, *not grudgingly* (II Corinthians 9:7). This expression literally means not "out of grief." Then Paul added, "nor of necessity." So many give because they feel they have to. "If I go to that service they'll take an offering," or "Here comes the plate. I'll have to put something on, much as it hurts me." A customer stopped in a drug store before church one Sunday morning, "Would you please give me two nickels for a dime?" Said the druggist, "Here you are and I hope you enjoy the sermon."

A funeral atmosphere prevails in most churches at offering time. Mendelssohn's *Consolation* would be appropriate offertory music to match the mood of people as they bid final farewell to their money. Perhaps anesthesia should be administered to make the extraction less painful.

However, Paul has something to say about the mood in which we give. When he commands us to give, not grudgingly, nor of necessity, he adds, "for God loveth a cheerful giver" (II Corinthians 9:7). The Greek word *cheerful* gives us our English *hilarious*. Offering time should be a happy occasion. To think of what God has done for us in Christ, and to realize that God, who owns all, has given us the opportunity of giving to Him, should make us cheerful, happy, hilarious givers. What a privilege! This is a most fitting time to say *Amen*. Some churches fittingly sing the Doxology as the ushers march down front with the filled collection plates to deposit them at the front.

Cursory contemplation of our countless blessings should keep us from acting like a little boy who was given a quarter and a dime one Sunday morning and told to put the quarter on the plate at church and to spend the dime on himself. Later on questioning he confessed, "I put the dime in church and spent the quarter on myself." Asked for an explanation he replied, "The preacher said the Lord loves a cheerful giver and I felt much more cheerful about putting a dime in."

A willingness to give pleases the Lord. When materials were needed for the tabernacle, "the Lord spake unto Moses, saying, Speak unto the children of Israel, that they bring me an offering: of every man that giveth it willingly with his heart ye shall take my offering" (Exodus 25: 1, 2). The result was that "they came, every one whose heart stirred him up, and every one whom his spirit made willing, and they brought the Lord's offering to the work of the tabernacle of the congregation" (35:21). In fact they gave so willingly that Moses had to restrain them from bringing any more gifts, for they had too much (36:6, 7).

The command not to become weary in well doing refers more to gifts than to works (Galatians 6:9), for the immediate context is dealing with sharing or giving. Churches whose people have stirred and willing hearts will respond cheerfully to financial appeals, and will not need money-raising schemes and ticket-selling to loosen money from tight wallets.

Ungrudging giving was insisted on by both the Old Testament and the Apocrypha. Regarding the poor, Moses said, "Thine heart shall not be grieved when thou givest unto him" (Deuteronomy 15:10). An extra-canonical book advised, "In every gift show a cheerful countenance" (Ecclesiasticus 35:11). The Rabbis said that cheerful kindness even if nothing were given was better than a morose gift. Someone has said, "Wrap your gift in a smile."

Incidentally, money giving is a good criterion of one's mental health. According to Dr. Karl Menninger, authority in the field, "Generous people are rarely mentally ill people." Misers are miserable, whereas the generous are joyful.

GIVING SHOULD BE GENEROUS AND SACRIFICIAL

Three boys were talking of their fathers and how much they earned. The first boy said his was a doctor and got $1,000 for an operation. Said the second, "That's nothing. My dad is a lawyer and often gets $2,000 for a case." The third boy, not to be outdone, piped up, "My dad's a preacher, and when he asks for money, it takes four men to collect it and carry it up front!" How wonderful if every legitimate appeal for the Lord's work received generous and sacrificial response. It has been said, "The only place for liberalism in the church is in the offering plate."

When King David was about to build an altar to

the Lord on the land of Araunah the Jebusite, the latter offered the threshing floor as a free gift, plus everything needed for the sacrifice on the altar. David sensed that to accept another man's gift and hand it over to the Lord would not be a sacrifice. Only something paid for with his own money involving denial would constitute a real sacrifice. Handing over fifty shekels, not a small sum, he said, "I will surely buy it of thee at a price: neither will I offer burnt offerings unto the Lord my God of that which doth cost me nothing" (II Samuel 24:24).

Yet how often we offer to the Lord that which costs us nothing. Malachi rebuked the people because they offered to the Lord blind, lame, and sick animals which were no good to the owners, thus no loss or sacrifice. Malachi reminds them they wouldn't offer sickly lambs to an earthly governor, so why palm them off on the Heavenly Ruler? Two little brothers were playing in the bathtub. They had a brand new, brightly painted Noah's Ark and were imagining the Flood. After the bath water was let out, one brother said, "Now we ought to do what Noah did — build an altar and offer a sacrifice." So dressing and taking some matches from the kitchen, they went outside, found some sticks and built an altar. But they needed animals to sacrifice. Looking at the nice animals in their ark, they felt they were too good to burn. "I know," said the other brother, "there's an old Noah's Ark in the attic." So he ran upstairs and returned with a little lamb which had two legs broken and the tail gone. Solemnly they placed the broken, useless lamb on the altar, offering that which cost them nothing.

A father tried to teach his seven-year-old girl the meaning of sacrifice. He explained that the finest gift a person can give is some cherished possession which he values a great deal. On his birthday he found pinned to his coat a large sheet of paper which his daughter had laboriously printed with red crayon, "You are my faverit Daddy and I luv you heeps. My present to you is what I likes best. It is in your poket." In his pocket he found a strawberry lollipop he had given her a week before. It hadn't been licked even once.

In our materialistic culture we know little of sacrifice. We don't feel it when we give. Our own comforts come before Lord's work. Little Mary Jane was walking to church with two nickels in her hand, one for the collection plate and one for herself. She tripped momentarily but as she regained her balance, she dropped one of her precious nickels. Before she could retrieve it the nickel rolled down a sewer. Looking down through the grating and coming to the sad conclusion it was lost forever, Mary Jane sighed, "There goes the Lord's nickel."

A missionary home on furlough was invited to a reception in his honor in a wealthy home where there were many well-to-do businessmen and finely dressed wives present. Later he wrote home, "Dear Wife: I've been entertained in a wonderful home. Prominent people were present. The women wore two chapels, one school, an organ and 1,000 books." The missionary, noting the wealth at home, could not help translating silks, satins, furs, finery and diamonds into needs on the field. Loaded with luxuries, we suffer no sacrifice. What we need is to decrease expenses and increase our offerings.

Zacchaeus lived for self and became rich. After Jesus paid him a visit, he gave away half of his goods, besides restoring fourfold to all he had defrauded. How many modern Christians today would consider giving away half of their assets?

When Mary realized that Jesus was heading for the cross, she took a costly box of alabaster, equivalent to a year's wages, and anointed him with it. She hadn't used it on her own brother, Lazarus, when he died a little while before this. Do our gifts to our Master exceed in value our gifts to loved ones? Do we ever give an amount equal to a year's salary?

When some early saints sold their lands and houses and gave the proceeds 100% to the apostles to distribute to the needy, they gave sacrificially. How many people today ever sell all they own and give it 100% to the Lord's work?

John Calvin spent all his salary, beyond his own needs, for the poor and the entertainment of strangers. C. T. Studd, Cambridge graduate who for many years lived in a single room, cooking his own meals, gave five million dollars to foreign missions. A slip of paper was found after his death on which he had scribbled, "Gladly would I make the floor my bed, a box my chair, and use another box for a table, rather than suffer men to perish eternally for want of knowledge of Christ."

A farmer saved $2,000 toward a new tractor. He almost closed a deal by which he was to get a new one with the money saved, plus his old one, which was almost falling apart. A letter came from a missionary friend telling of $2,000 needed for a new Bible school. After a hard struggle, he sent the money to Africa. Two years later he showed a visitor pictures of the new Bible school in Africa. "What about your tractor," asked the visitor. "Why," replied the farmer, "that old tractor still runs well!" The visitor quietly lifted his heart to the Lord, "O God, if only we all gave as sacrificially."

The difference between a collection and an offering is seen in the story of the boy who, when eating a pork chop dinner at home, filled up a plate with three pork chops to take out to his dog. His mother spotted him filling up this plate on the floor by his side, took the good meat away from the plate, and substituted bones. Taking the bones out to Towser, the boy lamented, "I had an offering for you, but now it's only a collection." Many people tip God when they should be tithing; many give a pittance when they should be offering plenty.

The Bible encourages generous giving. "He which soweth sparingly shall reap also sparingly; and he which soweth bountifully shall reap also bountifully" (I Corinthians 9:6). Jesus said, "Give, and it shall be given unto you; good measure, pressed down, and shaken together, and running over, shall men give into your bosom. For with the same measure that ye mete withal it shall be measured to you again" (Luke 6:38).

When Billy Graham visited Korea after the Korean War, he noted that refugees in Seoul, living in flimsy shelters in abject poverty and near starvation, with little children barefoot in the icy cold, had raised among themselves more than $8,000 to build a new church. When he asked, "How could you who have so little do all that?" a spokesman answered, "When we came here, we had nothing. God gave us some through the year and kept us going. And so we thought if God could start us with nothing and keep us through one year, we could start again with nothing and trust Him for another year!" A poor working man asked how he could give so much to the church replied, "I shovel out; God shovels in; and God uses the bigger shovel."

If someone wants to give sacrificially, he should not be denied the privilege. A church with very poor members gave large gifts to a church in another state whose people lost nearly everything in a flood disaster. The society handling the gift was reproached for taking these large gifts from the poor church. The society's treasurer replied, "Did the Lord tell the widow to come back and take even one of her two mites out of the treasury box?"

> "What can we spare?" we say.
> "Ah, this and this
> From mine array I am not like to miss;
> And here are crumbs to feed some hungry one.
> They are but in the way upon the shelf."
> And yet, one reads, our Father gave His Son!
> Our Master gave Himself.

GIVING SHOULD BE INTELLIGENT AND EXPECTANT

An observer of Hindu festivals reports how, while walking along the Ganges, he saw worshipers sacrifice money to the sacred stream. Copper coin in abundance would be tossed in by the common people who never handled higher values. Sometimes rich devotees would set out from the shore in curtained boats from which in midstream they would drop silver rupees or gold sovereigns to the mysterious current. But God is not honored by religious waste. He wishes our giving to be intelligent.

We shall be responsible not only for *what* we give but to *whom*. Careless, prayerless giving will come under divine scrutiny, because religious rackets have flourished through support from serious-minded people who should have investigated the object of their charity. Today's generous Christian public, enjoying unprecedented financial prosperity, too often becomes gullible prey for anyone who happens along with a plausible story which can be so quickly and vividly propagated by our modern, highly developed mass communication media. Intelligent giving demands careful investigation and spiritual discernment. Unless God's people give with caution, they may be pouring money into the pockets of unscrupulous self-appointed prophets who live high, wide, and handsome at the expense of tender-hearted saints. Our consecrated coin should go only to projects worthy of support.

We should give with expectancy, believing that our dollars will be translated into spiritual wealth. Children will be in heaven through the Sunday school and youth groups. People will be won to Christ. The saints will be edified. Heathen in foreign fields will some day be in glory. With faith we should deposit money on the plate. The schools we support, the radio programs we help, the organizations to which we contribute should transmute our gifts into eternal dividends.

God is rich, but God is poor. He owns the cattle on a thousand hills; the gold and silver are His. Yet He has limited Himself to the degree to which we loosen the strings of our purse. When a missionary needs the fare to sail to Africa, God does not rain down dollar bills to cover the cost. Though He owns all, He has committed the use of His possessions into the hands of His creatures.

A man with average income was challenged to share the support of a missionary in China. Though his wife and he didn't see how it could be done, they decided to send the $100 a month, a considerable sum a few decades ago. This they continued for several years, often receiving letters, curios, and personal visits from the missionary during furlough. The missionary told of souls won, a Bible school and local church established. The missionary died and was buried on Chinese soil. One day a letter came from a Chinese in which he told of his ancestry, his meeting with the missionary, and his conversion. His closing paragraph went something like this: "Now I give you a testimony for Jesus. God gives me peace and joy all the time. He supplies my needs. I can find no friend like Him. When I was tempted, He rescued me. When I was sick, He made me better. He answers prayers. He gives me courage to testify to others. How great is His love and mercy." He signed his name with the greeting, "in Christ." Said the American couple, "The sacrifice of all the years can't compare with the delight of seeing our money yield spiritual dividends."

> Walking down the Avenue
> She scans the luxury shops —
> Their rich display of beauty —
> And then she stops
> Entranced by mink or sable,
> By pearls, or diamond clip,
> Orchids in florists' windows
> Where scented fountains drip;
> Baskets of fruit and candy,
> Pale frocks of silk and lace,
> Sheer hose and cobweb lingerie —
> Of penury no trace. . . .
> Beyond the glittering windows,
> Beyond this sumptuous fare
> She sees the map of China,
> And the unsaved heathen there.

GIVING SHOULD BE NOT UNTO MEN BUT UNTO THE LORD

A visitor in a large New York city church reached into his wallet at offering time and chose a five-dollar bill. Suddenly he noticed that the usher coming his way was a millionaire known the country over. Wishing to make a good impression, he switched the five-dollar bill for a hundred-dollar bill, and placed it on the plate. He was giving as unto man.

A professional money-raiser stated that a strong motive for giving by many is the desire for prestige and the fear of public opinion. Motives haven't changed much since the time of Jesus, who condemned the Pharisees for making gifts just to be seen of men. "Take heed that ye do not your alms before men, to be seen of them: otherwise ye have no reward of your Father which is in heaven. Therefore when thou doest thine alms, do not sound a trumpet before thee, as the hypocrites do in the synagogues and in the streets, that they may have glory of men. Verily I say unto you, They have their reward" (Matthew 6:1, 2). The verb "to be seen" gives us our English word *theater*. The word "hypocrite" means an actor. Many people who give are just acting out a pretense, playing to the grandstand for effect. Our Lord gave a humorous picture here. Put it in a modern setting and picture a man sitting quietly in church until offering time. Then, as the usher reaches him, the man stands up for all to see, suddenly pulls a trumpet out from under his coat, gives a few staccato blasts to attract full attention, then while all are looking drops a $20 bill on the plate.

Our Lord, never a mere alarmist, gave this warning against such a practice — "Take heed." For if our purpose in giving is to make an impression on men, then when men have seen us and inwardly say, "What a generous man," we have what we wanted and thus we have our full reward. We have given unto men, not unto the Lord, so will receive no reward in heaven. Rather than give for show, we are told to "let not thy left hand know what thy right hand doeth" (Matthew 6:3).

Ananias and Sapphira gave to be seen of men. Impressed by others who were selling their houses and lands and giving the entire proceeds to the apostles, this couple sold their property, then bluffed the impression that they were giving 100% of the sale price to the apostles, while all the time keeping part for themselves. To retain part for themselves was their right, but not while leading men to think they were donating everything. They gave to be seen by people and were struck dead by the Lord. Someone has said that if the same fate befell all who were guilty of mixed motives in giving in our modern church, few people would be left.

The day the poor widow gave her two mites, rich men were ostentatiously dropping large sums in the offering receptacles. But her seemingly unnoticed gift, minute as it was, did not go unobserved by the divine eye, nor will it go unrewarded.

When entertainment marathons are televised to raise large sums for such causes as cerebral palsy, the full total of money promised by telephone is never realized. Phoning in gifts are people who like to hear their names given mention but who have no intention of paying up. When an offering plate is passed through a congregation row by row, total proceeds usually outweigh the gifts that would have been received if a plate had been placed at the door. People feel more compunction to give when a plate is passed in front of them while dozens of others are staring at them. But a gift given just to be seen of men is as worthless as the donation received in a letter to the Community Fund which read, "Gentlemen: Enclosed find my check for $2. You'll pardon me for not signing it, but I want to remain anonymous — A Friend."

Paradoxically, the person who gives to be seen of men may have his gift go unnoticed and receive no reward either in heaven or on earth, whereas one who gives unto the Lord with no concern as to whether or not he is seen by men, may have his gift unintentionally noticed so that he receives not only reward in heaven, but also recognition on earth, unsought though it was.

A missionary was asking for funds for his work. An old friend said, "Well, I'll give you $25, seeing it's you." The missionary replied, "No, I can't take anything for this cause, seeing it's I," and handed back the money. The man recognized the correctness of the reproof and quickly said, "You're right. Here's the $25, seeing it's for the Lord."

One night during an appeal for money, a little lame girl walked slowly up the aisle, leaning heavily on her crutch. At the front she pulled a ring from her finger and laid it with the many other gifts. Adjusting her crutch, she returned to her seat. After the service the preacher said to her, "My dear, I saw what you did tonight. It was beautiful, but you know, the response has been so large that we want you to have your ring back." The little girl looked up and firmly said, "I didn't give that ring to you."

A lady began to doze in church just before the offering. In her sleep she could see the ushers coming down the aisle. She reached reluctantly for a bill. The usher reached her seat. She was about to place the dollar on the plate. As she looked, the plate seemed to fade out. In its place was a nail-pierced hand waiting to receive her gift. Glancing up, she saw not the usher's familiar face but a face of deep tenderness and a thorn-crowned brow. For the first time in her life, it dawned on her that she was not giving to the usher nor to the church but to the Lord Jesus Christ.

> Give as you would if an angel
> Awaited your gift at the door;
> Give as you would if tomorrow
> Found you where giving was o'er.
> Give as you would to the Master
> If you met His loving look;
> Give as you would of your substance
> If His hand the offering took.

Luther is quoted as saying, "A man needs three conversions, first of the heart, then of the head, and lastly, of the purse." This final conversion will more easily take place if we contemplate often Christ's love-gift of Himself on our behalf. "For ye know the grace of our Lord Jesus Christ, that, though he was rich, yet for your sakes he became poor, that ye through his poverty might be rich" (II Corinthians 8:9).

When Money Turns Mute

6

When Money Turns Mute

Money can buy many things. A few extra dollars slipped under the counter into the hands of the proper party can often secure an extra favor. Money talks. But its power is generally limited to tangible objects, whereas it is often powerless to buy intangible values.

Under the caption, "The Alphabet Applied," a church bulletin listed these two columns side by side:

What Money Can Buy	What Money Cannot Buy
Autos	Ancestry
Bonds	Bliss
Clothes	Character
Dishes	Devotion
Entertainment	Equality
Flowers	Friendship
Gasoline	Gratitude
Horses	Health

The lists continued to the end of the alphabet, each tabulating twenty-six items.

A popular song writer of other years declared, "The Best Things in Life Are Free." Every morning and evening God paints a beautiful sunrise and a breath-taking sunset in His unique, unsurpassable brilliance, often with feathery, floating clouds. Could man create such works of art, he would fence them in and charge admission to view them. But God gives performances twice daily without cost.

In his *Travels With a Donkey*, Robert Louis Stevenson relates how, when camping out alone in a pine forest high in southern France, he exulted in the quiet joy of a wide starry sky. Still full of the wonder of the place as he packed to leave in the morning, he felt constrained to leave an offering for the overnight hospitality. Laughingly he dropped a few coins on the ground as he moved away, until he had left the equivalent of a night's lodging.

John Calvin, who disdained riches but who delighted in the beauty with which God had filled His world, wrote in the preface of Olivetan's New Testament in 1535, "The little singing birds are singing of God; the beasts cry unto Him; the elements are in awe of Him; the mountains echo His name; the waves and fountains cast their glances at Him; grass and flowers laugh out to Him." The glories of the creation are preferable to and unpurchasable by the gold of earth.

As a group of men were discussing various subjects, someone tossed out the well-known cliche, "Money can buy anything." A wealthy merchant impulsively offered $5,000 to anyone who could name just four covetable things which money could not buy. Little believing anyone could meet the challenge, he smiled confidently when one man took out his pencil and began to write. After scribbling four short lines, the challenger passed the paper to the merchant. He glanced at it carelessly at first, then gave it a more concentrated look. Within a minute he took out his checkbook to keep his promise. The paper listed these four items: a baby's smile; youth after it is gone; the love of a good woman; entrance into heaven.

Spurgeon told of a visitor who, seeing Bishop Hall of Waltham's large family, remarked, "These are they that make a rich man poor." "Nay," replied the bishop. "These are they that make the poor man rich!" The Bible says, "Children are an heritage of the Lord" (Psalm 127:3).

Someone wrote, MONEY WILL BUY —

> A bed but not sleep.
> Books but not brains.
> Food but not appetite.

Finery but not beauty.
A house but not a home.
Medicine but not health.
Luxuries but not culture.
Amusements but not happiness.
A crucifix but not a Saviour.
A church but not a heaven.

An English newspaper offered a prize for the best definition of money. The winner wrote, "Money is the universal passport for everywhere except heaven, and the universal provider for everything except happiness." There are some things money cannot buy. Sometimes money loses its might and becomes mighty mute.

MONEY CANNOT BUY HEALTH

Money is a must for purchasing food, which is in turn essential to good health. Visits to the local supermarket consume a major percent of the family budget. But funds haven't at all times and in all places been able to furnish nourishing or even necessary food.

In San Francisco during the 1849 gold rush apples sold for $125 a bushel, baked beans $1 a plate and eggs $1 each. When Rickenbacker and his friends were adrift in the South Pacific for days during World War II, their money did no good. There were no counters from which to select food, no corner grocery store to phone. One could starve to death in the Sahara Desert with a pocket full of $100 bills.

Nor can money guarantee the ability to enjoy food. A young business man strove hard to climb the ladder of success, often limiting his noon meals to a half hour or less to forge ahead. He frequently longed for a luscious steak but had neither the money nor the time. The day came when he was promoted to a top executive position and a two-hour noon lunch period. But by that time he had worked so hard that his doctor limited him to a toothpick and water for lunch!

This type of frustration the wise man had apparently observed: "A man to whom God hath given riches, wealth, and honour, so that he wanteth nothing for his soul of all that he desireth, yet God giveth him not power to eat thereof, but a stranger eateth it: this is vanity, and it is an evil disease" (Ecclesiastes 6:2).

A millionaire walking down the street saw a boy eating a crab apple. "I'd give half my fortune," he reputedly exclaimed, "to have a stomach like that boy!"

The wise man also wrote, "Every man also to whom God hath given riches and wealth, and hath given him power to eat thereof, and to take his portion . . . ; this is the gift of God" (Ecclesiastes 5:19).

Money cannot buy freedom from sickness. Financial resources may help prevent illness through proper medicines, and even in the hour of sickness provide the best medical and hospital care. Yet it cannot keep physical malady fully and finally away. There comes a day when all the world's wealth cannot effect a cure, like the woman of Jesus' day with the issue of blood who had spent all her living upon physicians, but could not be healed of any (Luke 8:43). Mrs. William Wrigley, Jr., who outlived her multi-millionaire husband by more than a quarter of a century, spent the last eleven years of her life in a coma. As far as conscious enjoyment of her millions, she was virtually a penniless pauper.

When we take our car to the garage, we can order a new tire, spark plug, battery, or even a whole engine. But when we take our body to the hospital for repairs, we cannot have new vital parts installed. Money cannot buy another heart, pair of lungs, kidneys, or eyes, though the day may come when limited transplants may be possible. To the lame man at the Beautiful Gate, Peter said, "Silver and gold have I none; but such as I have give I thee: In the name of Jesus Christ of Nazareth rise up and walk" (Acts 3:6). What this cripple needed money couldn't secure. Rather it came through the power of God.

Money cannot procure insurance against calamity. It

may secure insurance to cover damage done by fire, theft, or accident. A policy may be called comprehensive, but it can never be comprehensive enough to guarantee against the occurrence of disaster. Job was rich, yet catastrophes struck one after another. His oxen and asses were slain by the Sabeans. Lightning burned his sheep and servants. The Chaldeans fell on his camels and servants. A tornado destroyed his house and killed his sons and daughters. Finally disease covered his body.

Before boarding commercial airliners, many people take out $10,000 insurance by inserting 50¢ in the airport's insurance-vending machine, making it out to their prospective beneficiary. Financially sound as it may be, this insurance won't keep the plane from crashing. Should a plane begin a crazy careen to earth and should a millionaire passenger scream a promise of half his fortune to the pilot if he would land the plane safely, such a large sum multiplied several times could not prevent disaster.

When General MacArthur was forced to leave Corregidor in World War II, stacks of U.S. currency had to be left behind. To keep the money from falling into enemy hands, soldiers set the new $100 bills on fire. As the carton of bills melted into a blackened, burnt, shapeless mass, money never looked cheaper. Though the soldiers had "money to burn," it was mutely powerless to stave off military defeat.

Nor can money buy exemption from death. If it had this power, all rich men would live much longer and the middle-class and poor would die sooner. But the Lord regards not the rich more than the poor. In a moment shall they die (Job 34:19, 20).

The rich fool filled his barns with plenty and told his soul to take its ease. But that night death came in spite of his wealth (Luke 12:18-21).

Many rich have been willing to give thousands of dollars to extend life. Voltaire reputedly said on his deathbed to his physician, "I'll give you half of what I am worth if you'll give me six months of life!" Hobbes is supposed to have exclaimed, "If I had the whole world to dispose of, I would give it to live one day!"

All the money in the world can't keep the hearse from some day driving up to our door.

Money Cannot Buy Happiness

A savings bank motto read, "A full purse makes the heart light." However, millionaire Andrew Carnegie once said, "Millionaires seldom smile and never laugh."

Many who last night thought they were buying hilarious happiness woke up this morning with a hangover headache. Money can bring passing pleasure but no solid satisfaction. Although philosophers claim that you can't buy happiness, the American Institute of Public Opinion discovered through a recent poll that seven out of ten Americans felt that their happiness would be substantially increased if they could earn $37 more per week. Inflation, of course, would put a higher price tag on elusive happiness. A survey of 2,460 adult Americans conducted by the Joint Commission on Mental Illness and Health revealed that six out of ten worry most about money, three of whom insist that money is pivotal to their happiness.

Solomon, exceedingly rich, had an estimated annual income in our currency of roughly twenty million dollars, lived in a mansion which took thirteen years to build, drank from gold vessels, ruled from an ivory throne overlaid with gold, owned forty thousand stalls of horses for his chariots and had twelve thousand horsemen, sat down to a daily royal household menu which included one hundred sheep and thirty oxen, besides harts, roebucks, fallowdeer, and fatted fowl. If anyone were qualified to pass judgment on the ability of money and what it can purchase to satisfy the human soul, it was Solomon. Yet he concluded, "Vanity of vanities; all is vanity."

One object brings contentment for fleeting moments, then attention must be diverted to some other pursuit. Just before the coronation of Elizabeth II, a Texas millionaire cabled $1,500 to rent an apartment along the processional route. A London friend who was sent to check on the apartment wired back that the view was completely blocked by a grandstand. Came the millionaire's reply, "Buy the grandstand and tear it down!" Someone has said, "Rich people miss one of life's greatest thrills — paying the last instalment."

Had we the ability to turn whatever we touched into money, we should still be unhappy. King Midas, according to the old Greek legend, was cursed with an overwhelming love for money. The god Dionysius gave him the power to change everything he touched into gold. At first Midas went about touching all his possessions — chairs, bed, clothing — and was delighted as they turned into glittering gold. When his beloved daughter came running to greet him, his casual touch turned her into a golden statue. Love of money can change friends and family into frigid metal, sacrificing warm love for cold cash.

In fact, money can bring unhappiness. If acquired dishonestly, fear of detection will constantly haunt. Though winner of $129,000 on a rigged TV quiz program, Charles Van Doren before a congressional committee testified to a troubled conscience during the three years before he confessed his deception. If others know, the finger of scorn will be pointed in our direction. Zacchaeus, tax-collector made rich through dishonest practices, was miserably lost to himself, to others, and to God. "Better is a little with righteousness than great revenues without right" (Proverbs 16:8).

If wealth is honestly gained, complications often arise. "How can I protect my money?" "Will thieves make an attempt on my home?" "Are my stocks good?" These questions and a half dozen others will hound the rich. As income increases, expenses rise. Often people are so wrapped in their investments they forget spiritual matters. If not snared and drowned in riches, others trust wealth and feel no need of spiritual help, forgetting how poor they are before God. The ruler of Hyberabad, an Indian state, is said to have everything. The Nizam, as he is called, rules an area almost the size of Great Britain with more than 18 million population. His jewelry collection alone is valued at two billion dollars. Because he is a devout Moslem, he is limited to four legal wives. However, he has a harem of forty-two, plus fifty children. Yet he is also called the "Miser of Hyderabad." He waits in his bath while his one white suit is being washed or patched. He drives old cars and lives in a shabby palace. When a daughter was married, wedding celebrations were far below the expected, lavish, Oriental standards. Happiness consists not in the abundance of things a man possesses.

"Speak to my brother that he divide the inheritance with me" (Luke 12:13) is a plea heard in every century. Arguments over inheritances have broken many families. The peaceful town of Perryopolis, near Pittsburgh, became rich overnight in August 1948 when an eccentric widow willed it over a million dollars. At first people called it "Cinderella Town." But as the months passed, dissension as to how the money should be spent rent the town into violent strife. People who had been friends for years found themselves on opposite sides of the issue and wouldn't speak to each other. The bitterness waged for months and even years.

This Perryopolis incident bore close resemblance to Mark Twain's piece of fiction, The Man That Corrupted Hadleyburg, in which a stranger willed a fortune in gold to a reputedly guileless town on the condition that the man who had done some kindness to him years before would identify himself. Practically every important person in the town talked himself into believing he was the deserving heir. Gradually, the supposedly incorruptible town was almost irretrievably rent by wrangling.

Every man, woman, and child in the obscure Italian village of San Marco d'Urri was given 25 shares of Bank of America stock worth $1,200 in November 1959. Two brothers had sent the money from America in honor of their father who had spent his youth in San Marco. One widow refused her share, violently claiming this gift was the work of the devil and persuading her son and daughter to surrender their shares too. The village soon began to squabble over their new wealth. Not only did young fellows swagger around in new trench coats, not only was the peace of the countryside broken by the roar of scooter bikes, but a debate arose over what kind of "thank you" San Marco should give. "Change the name of the village to that of the donors." This was thought too cheap. "Erect a statue," but the village had no square. "Build a church in the upper part of the village in honor of the donors." But the residents of lower San Marco objected, suggesting a statue in front of the present church in their section. When a lad hit upon the bright idea of a statue halfway between the upper and lower areas, all agreed. Even the widow agreed, but when she sent her daughter out to claim her share of the stock, the daughter was caught in a sudden snowstorm and barely made it back to the widow who resumed her wailing, "This money is of the devil." *Newsweek* magazine began its report of this incident with the question, "Does money bring happiness?"

Money can't bring happiness in the hour of tragedy. Does an incurably sick man hug his bank book to his heart? Does a dying man call for his stocks and bonds? In the hour of sorrow, do dollar bills make the best handkerchiefs to dry one's tears? Money which looms so large in the hour of smooth sailing, dwindles to little consequence in the face of death. Money, like cargo, is mentally thrown overboard in the time of storm.

A man whose greed drove his wife and children out of his life lay dying in a hospital. To a visiting minister he confessed, "I don't have a friend on earth. I have thousands of dollars, but dollars cannot buy love." The man who at fifty is ten times richer than he was at thirty is not ten times happier. The unhappy poor fare better than the unhappy rich. The poor cling to the hope that money would terminate their unhappiness, whereas the rich know better.

Real joy consists not in having, but in being and doing — being right with God and doing His will. Not what we have but what we are makes life worthwhile. A rich man sought out his minister to ask him why he was so unhappy. The minister led him to a window and asked him what he saw. "People," the rich man answered. Then the minister pointed him to a mirror. "Now what do you see?" The man replied, "Myself." Then the minister explained. "Like the mirror, the window is made of glass. But the mirror's glass has a veneer of silver on it. As soon as silver is added, you don't see others — just yourself." Selfish people are never happy folks. The unselfish Paul could write, "As poor, yet making many rich; as having nothing, and yet possessing all things" (II Corinthians 6:10). Matthew Henry wrote, "I would think it a greater happiness to gain one soul to Christ than mountains of silver and gold to myself."

Reading the evening paper after supper in their beautiful home in New York City, a wealthy lady said to her husband, "I hear they're doing a good work down at Jerry McAuley's mission. Let's go down and help them." They found the mission full, so they sat at the rear. As they listened to the testimonies of the men who one by one told how God had rescued them, a new world opened to the rich couple. Finally, the wife whispered, "I guess they'll have to help us instead of our helping them. They've got something we haven't." Later when the invitation was given for those who wanted to accept Christ to come forward, this finely dressed pair responded and knelt at the altar in the sawdust beside drunken men and outcasts of the waterfront, and there they found real riches.

MONEY CANNOT BUY THE HOLY SPIRIT

After Simon the Sorcerer had professed faith in Christ, he was amazed at the signs and wonders Peter performed. When he offered to buy this power with money, he was soundly rebuked by the apostle, "Thy money perish with thee, because thou hast thought that the gift of God may be purchased with money" (Acts 8:20). The sin of trying to purchase spiritual power with money has been named after this sorcerer — *simony*.

Mary's magnificat contains this observation, "The rich he hath sent empty away" (Luke 1:53). The filling and the fruits of the Holy Spirit have no connection with money. Holiness and growth in grace are not produced by payment of dollars. No sales counter exists where one can exchange a $20 bill for unselfishness, patience, longsuffering, gentleness, self-control, meekness, or love of enemies.

Strong Christian character is the result of diligent application of one's entire personality and energies to the means God has placed at our disposal: feeding on the Bible, prayer, self-denial, death to the old nature and resurrection to the new nature, fellowship with Christian people, and obedience to the commands of God. It does not flourish overnight, much less is it bought with money, but it habituates through consistent consecration.

Sometimes church members seem to act as if a regular gift to the church excuses them from the duty of soulwinning, and a faithful contribution to the missionary fund takes the place of intense personal interest in and prayer for the missionaries. Their attitude is, "We pay the preacher and support the missionaries; let them do all that work." But the deeper life can never be replaced or replenished by dollars and cents.

MONEY CANNOT BUY HEAVEN

Some conscienceless judges can be bribed. Greasing their palm may bring respite from judgment. But the Judge of the universe cannot be bought. All the wealth of Egypt could not have stopped God's punishment on Pharaoh, the death of the firstborn, nor the drowning of the soldiers in the Red Sea.

God's chosen people were warned in ancient times, "Neither their silver nor their gold shall be able to deliver them in the day of the Lord's wrath" (Zephaniah 1:18). Also, "They shall cast their silver in the streets, and their gold shall be removed; their silver and their gold shall not

be able to deliver them in the day of the wrath of the Lord"
(Ezekiel 7:19). Captivity wasn't halted by currency.

Fabulous Farouk of modern Egypt couldn't stave off
the wrath of his people. In spite of his reputed multi-
millions, he was forced to flee. He now lives in exile while
his former properties are used as tourist accommodations.
Much less can dollars delay doom in the hereafter.

Nor can money buy forgiveness of sins. For we are
"not redeemed with corruptible things, as silver and gold,
. . . but with the precious blood of Christ" (I Peter 1:18,
19). The richest millionaire is too poor to purchase the
remission of his iniquities. The price was the sacrifice of
the sinless Saviour. Jesus paid it all.

Though money is indispensable in buying a home on
earth, it cannot buy a home in heaven. On the contrary,
the love of money may keep from heaven. The rich young
ruler went away from Christ because he had great wealth
which he wasn't willing to surrender for Christ. Inordinate affection for money lost him a home in heaven.

Our heavenly home, unprocurable through dollars and
cents, is a gift of God through Jesus Christ. Some men
have bought tickets to most major countries on earth and
were never refused admittance because they had sufficient
funds. But the same men at life's end will be barred from
heaven unless their hearts have been humbled, repentant,
and they turned in faith to Jesus Christ. They will be like
the old Indian chief in Texas who went to a railroad station to buy a ticket. He offered wampum and beads in
payment. When the agent refused him the ticket, he was
very indignant. He protested, "I'm the richest man in the
tribe and I can't buy a ticket over your railroad!" Though
rich at home, he was poor among civilized men. Currency
of this world is unacceptable for heavenly homes.

Respite from judgment, remission of sins, residence in
heaven — these cannot be claimed over the counters of com-
merce even with all the world's capital. The invitation to
heaven bears no price tag. "Ho, everyone that thirsteth,
come ye to the waters and he that hath no money; come

ye, buy, and eat; yea, come buy wine and milk without money and without price" (Isaiah 55:1).

The hymn writer expressed it aptly,

> When you look at others with their lands and gold,
> Think that Christ has promised you His wealth untold;
> Count your many blessings, money cannot buy
> Your reward in heaven, nor your home on high.

Patrick Henry wrote in his will,

> I have now disposed of all my property to my family. There is one thing more I wish I could give them, and that is Christian religion. If they had that, and I had not given them one shilling, they would have been rich; and if they had not that, and I had given them all the world, they would be poor.

A periodical published in England over a century ago carried the story of a man who took his own life when the bank in which he had invested all his capital failed. Following the story of the suicide the following anonymous rhyme was printed. Though no more than doggerel, this piece does point to the source of real riches.

> 1) Should all the banks of Britain break,
> The Bank of England smash;
> Bring in your note to Zion's bank,
> You'll surely have your cash.

> 2) And if you have but one small note,
> Fear not to bring it in;
> Come boldly to this bank of grace,
> The Banker is within.

> 3) All forged notes will be refused;
> Man's merits are rejected;
> There's not a single note will pass,
> That God has not accepted.

> 4) 'Tis only those beloved of God,
> Redeemed by precious blood,
> That ever had a note to bring —
> To this firm bank of God.

5) Tho' thousand ransomed souls may say
   They have no notes at all,
   Because they feel the plague of sin,
   So ruined by the fall —

6) This bank is full of precious notes,
   All signed, and sealed, and free;
   Though many doubting souls may say,
   There is not one for me.

7) The leper had a little note —
   "Lord, if Thou wilt, Thou can!"
   The Banker cashed his little note,
   And healed the sickly man.

8) We read of one young man, indeed,
   Whose riches did abound;
   But in the Banker's book of grace,
   His name was never found.

9) But see the wretched dying thief,
   Hang by the Banker's side;
   He cried, "Dear Lord, remember me,"
   He got his cash — and died.

A tax assessor was interviewing a godly, elderly widow whose cottage and little plot of land gave every evidence of poverty. She declared, "I am very rich." Taking out his book, the assessor said, "Please list your possessions." The widow replied, "I have, first, eternal life; second, a mansion in heaven; third, joy unspeakable and peace that passeth understanding." The assessor put away his book, sighing, "You are indeed a rich woman but none of your riches are taxable." Neither were her riches purchasable.

He who has Christ is rich indeed. Though health fail, some day he will have a perfect body. The joy of the Lord immeasurably surpasses evasive and evanescent happiness. To top it all, he possesses the prospect of a home in heaven where love shall be forever perfect and joy forever full. In the face of such blessings, money turns completely mute, for these cannot be bought but are freely available to all who link themselves by faith to Christ.

Where Will Your Money Spend Eternity?

7

Where Will Your Money Spend Eternity?

A rich man confined to his bed with an incurable illness enjoyed the company of his little girl who spent many
hours in his room, often visibly puzzled over why her big,
strong daddy was lying there so helplessly. One day his
business partners paid him a visit. The daughter somehow
sensed an air of finality about their call. When they left,
she inquired, "Father, are you going away?"

"Yes, dear, and I'm afraid you won't see me again."

Then the little girl asked, "Have you got a nice house
and lots of friends there?"

The father was silent for a moment, then turned con-
vulsively toward the wall, muttering, "What a fool I've
been! I've built a mansion here. I've made thousands of
dollars, but I shall be a pauper there!"

A man may die, leaving upwards of a million without
taking any of it upward.

Admittedly, giving has its present compensations.
Strange as it may seem, the person who receives a lovely
gift may be happy, but the one who gives is often happier.
We are so constituted that we find to be true a beatitude
of Jesus not recorded in the four gospels, "It is more blessed
to give than to receive" (Acts 20:35). The joy of acquisition is momentary and minute compared to the delights of
sharing. Satisfaction comes less from income than from
outflow. "Give, and it shall be given unto you; good
measure, pressed down, and shaken together, and running over, shall men give into your bosom. For with the
same measure that ye mete withal it shall be measured
to you again" (Luke 6:38). "Cast thy bread upon the waters:

for thou shalt find it after many days" (Ecclesiastes 11:1). "He that hath a bountiful eye shall be blessed" (Proverbs 22:9). Not only are givers enriched, but recipients, because their needs are thereby met, offer abundant thanksgiving to God for His goodness. Though giving sets up a network of reaction which yields recompense in the here and now, money presented with proper motive to the Lord's work also stores up spiritual treasure in the bank of heaven which will produce eternal dividends in the hereafter.

THE BANK OF HEAVEN

Missionaries tell how in Hong Kong imitation money across the top of which is written HELL BANK NOTE is sold by merchants to people whose loved ones have just died. Made to look like real money with a serial number and amounts up to $500,000 or other large denominations printed thereon, these notes are supposedly transferred to the deceased person's credit in the next world by burning them at the grave. They cost only a little and assure the departed ones of having some money in the world beyond. Sadly, it also tacitly admits they believe their loved ones are lost. While the Bible gives no justification for this pagan practice, the Scriptures do teach the possibility and desirability of a Christian sending on spiritual tender *in advance* of his departure from this life to his heavenly home.

When someone said, "George Washington threw a silver dollar across the Potomac," another added, "But dollars went further then." Dollars travel further when invested for eternity. Jesus commanded, "Lay not up for yourselves treasures upon earth. . . . But lay up for yourselves treasures in heaven" (Matthew 6:19, 20). To those who were persecuted for His sake, the Lord promised, "Great is your reward in heaven" (Matthew 5:12). The person who gave as small a thing as a cup of cold water as a disciple of Christ would not lose his reward (Matthew 10:42).

The judgment against the rich fool was, "He layeth up treasure for himself, and is not rich toward God" (Luke

12:21). It is possible to be rich on earth and poor in heaven. Jesus advised His followers not to invite for dinner people who in turn would invite them to their home for a meal and thus pay them back. Rather, He suggested that His followers invite those unable to pay them back, the poor, the maimed, the lame, and the blind, for then reward would come in the day of resurrection (Luke 14:12-14).

Had the rich young ruler sold his possessions and given them to the poor, he would have had what Jesus called "treasure in heaven" (Mark 10:21). "He that hath pity upon the poor lendeth unto the Lord" (Proverbs 19:17). When a certain king gave liberally to the poor, a relative rebuked him. "Your ancestors increased their riches, but you waste them." The king replied, "My fathers laid up wealth on earth; I lay mine up in heaven."

We need banks and brokers on earth. As pointed out in an earlier chapter, Christian responsibility demands providing for one's family. This will involve, among other items, insurance, a medical plan, and saving for children's college education. Also, it does not seem inconsistent with Christian stewardship for a believer to have a financial program for retirement, prudent forsight for a "rainy day," and investments for some particular ambition like a trip to a foreign country. But each Christian must be able to justify these expenses in his conscience before God. Certainly God would have us invest our money most wisely. Thus we need banks and brokers.

But this chapter protests against the practice of piling up wealth in earthly banks with no thought of the bank of heaven. How quick people are to invest money in property, stock, bonds, and banks down here! How reluctant many are to invest in the Lord's work! Many, when making a gift, unconsciously leave the impression that they will never see it again. Inwardly they change the words of the hymn to "God be with you, for we'll never meet again." For all practical purposes, they may as well be dropping their contribution into a sewer or tossing it into a garbage can. To them it's gone and gone forever. A little boy who had no offering at a children's meeting explained, "My mother didn't give me any because she said she didn't want to waste her money." But the Bible teaches that the only money we shall meet again is that given with proper motives to the Lord's work. Paul exhorts the rich among other things to distribute, to be willing to share, "laying up in store for themselves a good foundation against the time to come" (I Timothy 6:18,19). In other words, they by giving deposit wealth in heaven's bank.

No preacher should apologize for speaking on money. A stockbroker who leads people to invest wisely in earthly enterprises does them a big favor. Similarly, every preacher is really a spiritual financial salesman, urging people to invest in the Lord's business and helping them to have treasure eternally. Besides, he prompts them to focus their attention on things above, for what you get your interest from is what you'll have your interest in. Or as Jesus put it, "Where your treasure is, there will your heart be also" (Matthew 6:21). Moreover, the promoter of heavenly investments has this advantage over earthly brokers — he pushes a bank that will never fail, whereas terrestrial companies can collapse.

Though we can't take our money with us when we die, we can send it on ahead. A well-to-do church member was showing a visiting minister around his estate. Later they stood on a second-floor outside balcony, surveying the scenery. "As far as you can see to the north, that's mine!" said the rich man to the minister. Then pointing to the west, "As far as you can see in that direction, I own!" Swinging to the south, then the east, he made the same claim. Quietly the minister pointed skyward and asked, "How much do you own up there?"

THE BANK OF HEAVEN IS SECURE, SOUND AND STABLE

Men look for safe and stable securities, but no material investment is fully secure.

Jesus spoke of the "deceitfulness of riches" (Matthew 13:22). Money misleads in many ways. It enslaves. An eagle, feasting on the dead carcass of an animal that was floating down the Niagara river in mid-winter, spread its wings to fly away as it came to the falls, but it discovered that its claws had become frozen in the carcass and it was swept over the wild cataract to destruction. The lure of easy money leads to wrongdoing. In 1960 five Moroccan merchants were sentenced to death for their get-rich scheme of selling for medicine a mixture of olive oil and jet-plane lubricant which permanently maimed 10,000 persons in that country. The love of money can also shrivel up the soul so that a man has everything he supposed he wanted and yet nothing that he really wants. Besides, it can trap people into depending on it as though it were all-powerful. Many unwittingly reason, "I have a good position. I have good health. I have lots to eat, a nice home, and a healthy bank account. I'm protected by ample insurance. Social security plus large retirement benefits will take care of me after I'm sixty-five. Everything is fine!" Though they would verbally affirm the existence of God, they live as though God did not exist, rarely thinking of spiritual matters and never darkening the door of a church except at Easter and Christmas. Paul told Timothy to warn the rich not to "trust in uncertain riches, but in the living God" (I Timothy 6:17). A major deceptive quality of money is that it leads people to attach permanence to it. Thus, because riches are uncertain, money lulls people into false security. Just as "permanents" for ladies' hair are misnamed, because they do not last, and so should rightly be termed "temporaries," so securities should more aptly be called "insecurities."

1. Decay

The ancients used to have their wealth in change of garments or in precious metals. Immense value resided in garments passed down from generation to generation. Jacob gave Joseph a coat of many colors. Joseph gave five changes of raiment to Benjamin. Achan wanted a Babylonian garment from Jericho. Samson promised thirty changes of garments to the one who guessed his riddle. Naaman gave five changes of raiment to the king of Israel. Christ promised white raiment to those who overcome. Wealth was hoarded up as raiment in the Orient. But in one night moths could reduce whole wardrobes of garments to shredded lace-work. Others saved gold and silver. But metals could rust. James prophesied, "Your gold and silver is cankered; and the rust of them shall be a witness against you" (James 5:3). In urging people to put their treasure in the bank of heaven, Jesus pointed out that this was a place "where neither moth nor rust doth corrupt" (Matthew 6:20).

How significant — a few decades back we could own all the gold we wanted to but no intoxicating liquor. Today we can have intoxicating liquor, but are forbidden to own gold!

2. *Thieves*

A seventy-year-old lady in New York City who had lost faith in banks carried $16,000 in bills and $15,000 in jewels in a black bag wherever she went. Shortly after midnight a few years ago, she entered a cafeteria near her hotel, carrying the black bag. She placed it on a chair and and tossed her coat over it. Then she began to look around the cafeteria. When she returned to her place, her coat was on the floor and her bag gone.

Frequently papers tell the stories of jewel and fur robberies in the apartments of the well-to-do. When you are rich, you become a potential target for blackmail, embezzlement, and kidnaping. One wealthy man owned two houses, and he kept them both guarded by burglar alarms and special locks, beside a full-time watchman. But in spite of armored cars, policemen, judges, locks, and alarms, money may be stolen. In pointing out the advantages of laying up treasures in heaven, Jesus said it was a place "where thieves do not break through nor steal" (Matthew 6:20).

3. Bank Failures or Stock Market Decline

The late Dr. R. A. Torrey told how when he was a boy he sat around the fireside one evening with his mother, father, and sisters, together totaling up the family wealth. As different properties were named, an estimated value was written down in a column. When the inventory was finished, the father said, "Add up the column and divide the total by five and you will see what you will be worth when I am gone." Dr. Torrey said that as a boy he felt quite rich thinking of all the money coming into his possession some day. But the financial panic of the 1870's came and swept away all his father's properties. "All I have left of the estate is a pair of cuff links and a match box."

Most people do not keep much money in their pockets or dressers but deposit it for safe keeping in the bank. Yet banks have been known to fail. When Czechoslovakia fell into the Russian orbit, the puppet government confiscated large sums of the people's money by simply claiming all the savings accounts in the banks of the country.

Oft related is the story of what happened to a group of our nation's most successful financiers who sat around a table in the Edgewater Beach Hotel in Chicago in 1923. They included:

The president of US Steel
The president of the largest utility company
The greatest wheat speculator
The president of the New York Stock Exchange
A member of the president's cabinet
The greatest speculator on Wall Street
The president of the Bank of International Settlements
The head of the world's greatest monopoly

Magazines for years had carried their success stories as examples for youth to follow.

But a roll call a quarter century later revealed the following startling facts:

The president of US Steel — Charles Schwab — lived on borrowed money the last five years of his life and died broke.

The president of the largest utility company — Samuel Insull — died a penniless fugitive from justice in a foreign country.

The greatest wheat speculator — Arthur Cutten — died insolvent.

The president of the New York Stock Exchange — Richard Whitney — had served time in Sing Sing Prison.

The member of the president's cabinet — Albert Fall — was pardoned from prison so that he could die at home.

The greatest speculator on Wall Street — Jesse Livermore — committed suicide.

The president of the Bank of International Settlements — Leon Fraser — committed suicide.

The head of the world's largest monopoly — Ivar Kreuger — committed suicide.

Stocks, bonds, banks, and corporations down here are liable to failure, but the bank of heaven is guaranteed not to fall.

4. Disaster

A service station owner began to store tires in his home basement, because he thought a tire shortage was imminent. While he was on vacation, his house caught on fire, burning all the tires in his cellar. A couple acquired a large freezer and loaded it with over $100 worth of meat and other provisions. Through some mechanical failure which they didn't discover for several days, the freezer went off and their food spoiled. Who knows when fire, earthquake, tidal wave, hurricane, tornado, or large doctor bill can wipe out wealth?

The government guarantees bank deposits for a few thousand dollars and stands behind US Treasury bonds. But any nation is vulnerable to nuclear attack and destruction. What value would our banks and bonds have then?

5. Death

Even if we could successfully maneuver the ship of our finances around the shoals of decay, dishonesty, bank failure, market drop or disaster, death will ultimately relieve us of our money. We bring nothing into the world and we take nothing out.

One word answers the perennial questions, "How much did he leave?" The answer, "Everything." There are no pockets in a shroud. It is said that when Alexander the Great died, his hands were left outside the coffin to show the viewers that though he had conquered the world, he carried nothing with him into the hereafter.

> Rake, scrape, borrow, and save —
> You lose it all when you go to the grave.
> Money, a dead man's hand won't hold,
> Nor can life be purchased with silver and gold.
> —*Author Unknown*

A preacher visited a middle-aged couple to talk about spiritual things. They virtually closed the door in his face with this excuse, "We have set as our goal the accumulation of investments which will enable us to soon retire comfortably and to build a beautiful new home. Both of us work. After a few years when we have saved all we need, we will come to your church." The years passed and the couple prospered. Their savings had reached a substantial figure and their new mansion-like home was nearly complete. The week before they were to resign their positions and move into their home, the husband, just fifty, dropped dead of a heart attack.

When a wealthy man passed away, someone remarked, "No man ought to be allowed to leave so much money." A friend replied, "You're a little hard on him. I was with him when he died, and let me assure you — he didn't want to leave it!" Some men do not leave their money. They are taken from it. But in heaven there is no death. The bank of heaven is rustproof, burglarproof, failureproof, stormproof, disasterproof, and deathproof.

How long does a dollar bill last? The average life of a bill is thirteen months. Too limp to circulate, it is tossed into the incinerator. Over a million dollar bills are burned every year. How long does a dollar bill last when exchanged for value? What we spend on food lasts a few hours. What we spend on clothing lasts a few years. What we spend on furniture or a home we enjoy for a few decades. What we spend for Christ lasts for eternity.

How to Make Deposits in the Bank of Heaven

Though we may soon be sending a man to the moon, we can't climb up to the bank of heaven. What chemistry can change earth's gold into heaven's coin? When one travels to a foreign country, he must change his money into the coinage of the new realm. How does one change earthly bills into heavenly money?

A man in Canada had a son in the United States. Canadian Foreign Exchange regulations prevented the father from sending money across the border. Wishing to purchase a book at a New York publishing company, the father wrote his son to this effect, "If you will take some of your money and order that book to be sent me, when you come to Canada this summer I'll have the money waiting for you." Similarly God says, "I want some work done on earth. I have no money. If you will take some of your money and use it for my wishes, then when you come up to heaven some day I'll have it waiting in your account."

A man gave several thousand dollars to help erect a church. Then came the crash. He lost all he had. Someone said, "If you had that money you gave to start the church, you would have enough to set yourself up in business again." He replied, "Sir, I would have lost that too in the crash. As it is, it's the only money I have saved. It is now in the bank of heaven yielding interest which will accumulate till eternity. Hundreds have come to know Christ through the church it built!"

John Bunyan wrote,

> A man there was,
> Some called him mad,
> The more he gave away,
> The more he had.

An old gravestone said,

> What I spend, I had;
> What I saved, I lost;
> What I gave, I have.

The miser has misery both here and hereafter —

> Throws up his interest in both worlds,
> First starved in this, then damned in that to come.

Someone else has said,

> Do your giving while you're living;
> Then you're knowing where it's going.

The first requisite to putting money in the bank of heaven is to open an account there. You cannot deposit money to your name in a bank if you have no account there. Proper procedure demands first arranging for an account. Similarly, to get credit for eternal treasure you must first have your name on heaven's register. To have your name on the Lamb's Book of Life, you must repent and turn in faith to the Lamb of God, trusting in His sacrifice on Calvary's cross for your redemption. Money given to the Lord by one who has not yet done business with the Lord means nothing.

After enrolling in heaven's register you can gain eternal wealth simply by giving to the Lord's work down here. Just as bountiful sowing means bountiful reaping, so generous giving here yields generous dividends hereafter. Financial support of Bible-teaching churches, Christian colleges, Gospel-preaching missionaries, and other evangelical organizations lays up treasure above.

Another way of storing up eternal wealth is to give to the poor. To the rich young ruler Jesus said, "Give to the poor, and thou shalt have treasure in heaven" (Mark 10: 21). Augustine said that after giving our tithe we could place money "in the heavenly treasure by way of alms to the poor."

It has been estimated that if the world population were compressed into a single town of 1000 people, about 700 would be ignorant, poor, sick, and hungry. Over 500 would never have heard the name of Jesus Christ, much less that He lived and died for their sins. Opportunities to lay up treasure in the bank of heaven are vast.

> You sent a dollar across the sea,
> That bought a Bible for Yong Sing Lee.
> And Yong Sing Lee, when he read therein,
> Decided to quit his life of sin.
> Then he rested neither night nor day
> Till his brother walked in the Jesus way.
> Now his brother worked until he won
> Away from their gods, his wife and son.
> Soon half of their neighbors and friends had thrown
> Away their dead idols of wood and stone.
> And the work is not finished yet, my friend,
> You started something that never will end,
> When you sent the dollars across the sea
> Which bought a Bible for Yong Sing Lee.

Not what we grab, but what we give, makes us rich. Or as Jim Elliot wrote in his diary before his martyrdom by the Auca Indians, "He is no fool who gives up what he cannot keep to gain what he cannot lose." Yet God's people squander millions of dollars every year on luxuries and vanities which could have been used to build churches, increase the salaries of teachers in Christian colleges, feed the hungry, send Christ's ambassadors to other continents, and thus bring eternal returns.

Suppose we were told that ten years hence nuclear war would invalidate our present currency. Our present coins and bills would no longer be acceptable. Suppose that what would make acceptable currency would be *pencils*. Property, stocks, bonds, money—all worthless; the only good medium of exchange — pencils. When preachers exclaimed, "Money will be worthless. Seek pencils. Lay up pencils against the day of tragedy," people would laugh and still go on saving money. But the thoughtful person would reason, "Why go on accumulating what will be valueless in ten years? I'll turn every dollar into pencils." With a slight twist, we have the Bible message. Money will be worthless in the world to come unless it has been transmuted into spiritual purposes. So don't hoard money. Give to the Lord's work and have the coin of heaven waiting for you above.

Sigmund Freud's favorite story concerned a sailor shipwrecked on a South Sea island, seized by the natives, carried shoulder-high to a rude throne and proclaimed king. He learned that according to their custom the king ruled for a year. The idea appealed to the sailor until he wondered what had happened to all the previous kings. Then he learned that when a king's reign ended, he was banished to a lonely island to starve to death. Knowing he was king for the year, the sailor began issuing orders. Carpenters were to make boats. Farmers were to go ahead to this island and plant crops. Builders were to erect a home. When his reign finished, he was exiled, not to a barren isle but to a paradise of plenty.

Our Lord said, "Make to yourselves friends of the mammon of unrighteousness; that, when ye fail, they may receive you into everlasting habitations" (Luke 16:9).

> The angels from their thrones on high
> Look down on us with wondering eye,
> That when we are but passing guests
> We build such strong and solid nests.
> But where we think to dwell for aye
> We scarce take heed a stone to lay.

A legend tells of a man who lived on the main highway through a busy town. One day an angel visited him with this message, "Some day the King of the Celestial City will call you to come and live with Him." He thought, "I must have the finest suit to wear when I enter His city. I must save my gold so I shall have money when I arrive there."

One snowy night there came a knock at his door. A stranger stood there in ragged clothes, his teeth chattering. "The King of the Celestial City has asked me to visit Him and I'm on my way, but I don't have any good suit to wear. Besides I'm shivering. I wonder if you could spare some clothes to keep me warm and help me look nice when I see the King." The man thought of his smart new suit but shook his head no, for thought he, "What would *I* wear when *I* go to see the King?"

The next night another knock came. This time a poor lady stood there. "Please sir," she sobbed, "I'm a widow. My husband died last year, leaving me with an only girl. She's so sick that only an operation can save her life, but I have no money for the doctor or the hospital. Could you loan me some gold? I would work hard to repay every ounce. Please help me." The man thought of his gold but turned the weeping woman away thinking, "What money would I have to buy things in the Celestial City if I gave her my gold?"

One day word came to this man that the King of the Celestial City wanted to see him. So he ran upstairs to don his new suit, but when he threw open his closet, he found that moths had eaten gaping holes in both coat and trousers. When he looked in his box for his gold, it had turned to brass. He had to make his trip to see the King in his moth-eaten suit and without any gold.

The next day he noted his neighbor approaching the Celestial City. He was likewise wearing an old suit and was penniless. But when he neared the gate, the King ran to meet him. The minute the King touched the neighbor, his worn suit was miraculously transformed into a handsome new suit and his pocket was immediately filled with gold pieces. When the man looked astonished at what was happening to his neighbor, the King explained, "That night you turned away the shivering beggar and did not give him your suit, he went next door to your neighbor and he gave him his finest suit. The next night when you refused to give any gold to the poor widow to save her sick daughter's life, your neighbor gave her the little gold he owned. You kept your treasure down there, but he sent his on ahead!"

In a vision, a couple were seen nearing the end of life's journey. They were lugging a lot of baggage, money, stocks, bonds, finery, jewels, and furs. Just outside the gate of the New Jerusalem was a junk pile. "Throw all your things in that heap," the angel ordered. Slowly, most reluctantly, the man and woman parted with their earthly treasures which they held so dear but which were worthless up above.

Another couple approached. Carrying very little baggage, they looked expectantly toward the gate, which swung outward as songs of praises rang within. A group of people were awaiting them whom they had never met. The angel explained, "These are they who have been won to Christ in distant lands through the money you gave to missions." Then the converted heathen thanked the newcomers, saying, "We were in darkness. One day missionaries came and told us of the Lord. That's why we're here. The great Saviour looked over His records and told us it was money you gave that sent the messengers out." Then together all praised the Lord Jesus Christ.

May not faithful giving to the Lord's work provide one reason some Christians will have an abundant entrance into the everlasting kingdom? (II Peter 1:11).

In Revelation, last book of the Bible, references to offerings are rare. The time will come when offerings are no more. So, the time to give is now — or never!